KU-600-297

ON DIRECTING

Interviews with Directors

edited by Gabriella Giannachi and Mary Luckhurst
foreword by Peter Brook

ff
faber and faber

First published in 1999
by Faber and Faber Limited
3 Queen Square London WC1N 3AU

Typeset by Faber and Faber Ltd
Printed in England by Clays Ltd, St Ives plc

All rights reserved

This collection © Gabriella Giannachi and Mary Luckhurst, 1999
Copyright in individual interviews belongs to the interviewers and the
individual interviewees
Foreword © Peter Brook, 1999

Gabriella Giannachi and Mary Luckhurst are hereby identified as editors of this
work in accordance with Section 77 of the Copyright, Designs and Patents Act 1988

*This book is sold subject to the condition that it shall not, by way of trade or otherwise,
be lent, resold, hired out or otherwise circulated without the publisher's prior consent in any
form of binding or cover other than that in which it is published and without a similar
condition including this condition being imposed on the subsequent purchaser*

A CIP record for this book
is available from the British Library

ISBN 0-571-19149-5

2 4 6 8 10 9 7 5 3 1

for Peter Holland

Contents

Acknowledgements

The editors would like to thank Baz Kershaw, Rachel Parslew, Steve Purcell, Jane Turner and Stephen Walton. Special thanks go to Nick Kaye and John Lennard for reading the interviews throughout the drafting processes and offering suggestions for their improvement.

At the time of writing, Mary Luckhurst was a Wingate Scholar at Cambridge University and is grateful to the Harold Hyam Wingate Foundation for their support both on this book and on her research work as a whole.

Foreword

The work of a director can be summed up in two very simple words: *Why* and *How*. The two words do not sit easily together. *Why* is both a small word and a gigantic concept. *Why* make theatre at all? Every director is drawn towards directing because, consciously or unconsciously, they have a certain vision, a certain dream; they have a certain task to make something marvellous and extraordinary, to do something that is beyond other jobs and ordinary life, in this strange place called theatre. As a director begins to work they move from the *why* do I want to be a part of this world? to the *how* can I make theatre? *How* can come down to small matters, whether they are solid, practical details or sordidly small things. But the director's role, whatever their school or style, is always to make a living link that betrays neither the small *why* nor the great *Why*; the small *how*, nor the great *How*.

In the world of *why* there are many everyday questions: *why* make theatre? *why* be a director? Is it because we want to earn our living in a pleasant way? Is it because it's more exciting, more engrossing than many other jobs? But unlike in most jobs, in theatre there is a romance, a sexuality, an immediacy, a vibrancy and an excitement. So on a small level the answer to why make theatre and why be a director is: because it's enjoyable. This is the small *why* and it's perfectly honourable to do a job and enjoy it, earning a living while looking after one's family. All this is honourable. It becomes dishonourable if, in the process of one's work, the larger *Why* is betrayed.

The larger *Why* relates to intuition, which tells us that any artistic form is an opening; an opening in which the *Why* is wide, wide-open, wide-eyed and opens onto perspectives that are normally closed. If the director becomes bored, or jaded or cynical, they lose the sense of the great *Why*: that *Why* in which the psychological, the social, the spiritual and the scientific all come together. That director remains with the small *why*, and the true *Why* is forgotten. How can a director remain in touch with the everyday and not lose the aspiration and love that was present at the beginning? How can a director sustain the great *Why* and remain in the world of *How* at the same time?

The world of *How* is the world in which the director is a craftsman; in which the director is responsible for bringing everything down to earth.

This involves such things as knowing the difference between two people on stage being close together or far apart; between a platform being high or low; between a taut and a sloppy tempo; between the lights being bright or dark; between the audience being able to participate or not participate; between a living response in the audience or the absence of a living response; and between the interest of the audience being shared or not shared with the actors. This is the large *How*. The small *how* may be a question of how an actor raises a finger and at what speed. If the larger *Why* is also present in the work then the simplest of details will carry a resonance and weight which will not be there if the director simply says: 'Well, *Why* can wait. Just now I'm dealing with the small matter of where to place a nail.' In fact, *How* and *Why* are inseparable.

Directing is only one century old. Those who first plunged into an exploration of this new world of 'directing' did so with the joy and enthusiasm of pioneers discovering new lands. There were some great figures amongst them, some of them more carried away by aspiration than practicalities; and others who were in tune both with their aspirations and the question of *How* to bring them about. There was Stanislavski, who was passionately interested in the human organism, this unknown creature out of which such mysterious things could come. He was interested in the creation of character both like the actor and not like the actor, a territory so mysterious that he felt it had to be examined closely and – above all – practically. There was also Gordon Craig, for whom the *Why* mattered above all else. Why a theatre experience at all unless it is to take the human being to the most exalted levels that the human spirit can reach? This great romantic dream inspired him so strongly that he ultimately preferred it to the mundane realities of the *How* and gave up production. Nonetheless, Craig's dream is a vital part of twentieth-century theatre. Then there was Artaud. Artaud led a passionate search not in the exalted areas of the human spirit but in the burning hell that is also part of human experience – yet he only directed about a dozen evenings of performance in his whole career. There were also Meyerhold and Brecht. Meyerhold was perhaps the greatest genius that theatre has ever known. He explored the psychological, behaviourist mechanism of the actor as well as all the attendant arts: the art of scenery; the nature of rhythm; the nature of music; the exact nature of text; the relation between a text and an audience; and the relation between performer and audience. All these methods, these systems belong to their moments and are rapidly carried away by time. But we can learn from all these practitioners. From Meyerhold, for example, we learn that the director must be cultivated, that he must investigate and know as many areas as he can possibly reach, in both the past and the present, in order to be well prepared for his function. This was Meyerhold's challenge; probing deeply into the human comes from Stanislavski; Craig appeals to us not to lose sight of the invisible world; Artaud demands a recognition of the painful, intolerable sides of human experience and warns against the comfort of beauty and romance; Brecht reminds us that the reality of the world outside the theatre is the same reality that the audience carry with them into the theatre, and that a director must face its urgent needs at every moment.

More than anything else, the example that these great figures bring to us is not their method but their passion. Every director starts from a different point in time and has to find their own way. But unlike philosophers and poets, directors are not alone: theatre, television and cinema are communal activities. Directors depend on and work with others, and these other people, the actors and audience, open up the search for us and allow us to go beyond our individual capacity. Directors never work alone: they function within a complex act of relationships and this is their strength. The *How* and *Why* of directing are formed by other people. The spectators do not have a secondary position, to buy or not buy; they are collaborators who allow the whole theatre experience to take on meaning. No rehearsal that I have ever attended can have the same quality as a true moment of performance, because it is the contribution of the audience that makes the experience whole. But the director can bring the passion that lights the fire.

It is essential to understand the history of the director. The early pioneers could not help feeling, like any inventor, that the new world belonged to them, and two myths evolved from this: the first is that the director is a dictator; and the second is that, although dictators are unattractive in all political spheres, the director of a play or film, the conductor of an orchestra, is entitled to be the supreme boss. Historically this is understandable, but today life has changed, and the art of directing has changed. Any director who sees the theatre as an enormous palate existing only for the production of their own personal conceptions, who views the whole complex machinery of theatre as the pen in their hand and the opportunity to write their own fantasies, is a loser. This is a view which belongs to the past. Today we perceive that if the director has a search, this search is animated by an undying sense of *Why* in relation to ever-changing human experience. That search is made real by the need of an appropriate craft, and this means recognizing constantly changing means. And because the means of theatre are always changing there can be no systems or schools of directing that last forever.

Directors, by the nature of their craft, have become more and more isolated from one another. There is a need to recognize that every director with their individual differences, approach and style – every one of which can be true and totally legitimate – belongs to a shared, international fraternity. We must seize every opportunity that offers the possibility of understanding and respecting each others' work, and enjoy the possibility of being influenced and changed by another director. We must watch and listen. Our attention and respect for one another is vital in an increasingly ruthless society.

[Edited extracts of a talk given by Peter Brook to the Directors Guild of Great Britain in 1996]

INTRODUCTION

In Britain the cult of the director dominates theatre practice; it is difficult to imagine a time when this was different. In fact the term 'director' is barely a hundred years old: before the late nineteenth century the overall artistic concept and responsibility for the staging of a play were dispersed amongst various figures in the company. Often decision-making for a performance lay with the troupe of actors, with the actor-manager or with the playwright, and historical sources indicate that sometimes stage managers and book-keepers also acted as supervisors of productions.

The established twentieth-century understanding of the director's role is conventionally traced back to the court theatre of Meiningen in Germany in the late nineteenth century. Here Ludwig Chronegk formed a partnership with Duke Georg II and founded an ensemble company that became legendary. As artistic director, the Duke gave the overall interpretation and visualization of the play, and Chronegk ran the company, conducted rehearsals and translated the Duke's ideas into stage action. The Meiningen Company productions broke radically with tradition in their emphasis on the rehearsal period and the importance of process: for the first time the actual *making* of the production became a vital part of the product itself. As a result rehearsals were prolonged, and a great deal of time was invested in researching design and costumes. Chronegk's rehearsal techniques and the new theatre aesthetic that resulted from them were a radical turning-point in the history of theatre practice, and it was not long before figures such as Konstantin Stanislavski and André Antoine were exploring them in their own theatrical experiments. From this point on, rehearsals acquired a central role in theatre-making, rehearsal and acting methods began to multiply, and the director was placed at the top of the theatre-making hierarchy.

The twentieth century has seen an explosion of directing practices; these include: the precise 'sciences' of directing as propounded by Stanislavski, Antoine and Otto Brahm; Vsevolod Meyerhold's theories of biomechanics and constructivism; Adolphe Appia and Gordon Craig's radical ideas on design and space; the 'epic theatre' of Bertolt Brecht; Antonin Artaud's 'Theatre of Cruelty'; Jerzy Grotowski's 'poor theatre'; Peter Brook's explorations of 'the empty space'; Augusto Boal's 'Theatre of the Oppressed'; the 'Living Theatre' of Julian Beck and Judith Malina; the Wooster Group's avant-garde multimedia work; Robert Wilson's formal aesthetic; Ariane Mnouchkine's 'Création collective' and the dance theatre of Pina Bausch and Meredith Monk. These are just a few famous names and there are many others.

In Britain the play-text has traditionally been privileged above the visual, physical and spatial elements in theatre. The modernist experiments, which had a profound impact on the development of theatre in Central and Eastern Europe, were slow to leave their mark on British theatre, and as a result the first series of significant challenges to the orthodoxy of text-based theatre came in the 1960s. Companies and individuals questioned the conventions of British theatre in a multitude of ways. They overturned received ideas about the locus and duration of a performance, the privileging of rhetorical delivery over physical agility for performers and the hierarchization of written narrative above narratives of space, time, visual effects and the body. Many sought to combine different art forms and experimented in performance art. Many were consumed with, and others entertained, questions of political activism, seeking to galvanize audiences through events and actions. Many turned to issue-based theatre, others to community projects. At the base of this multi-scale interrogation there were fundamental queries surrounding the nature and purpose of theatre itself. The processes of theatre and performance making were scrutinized, alternative practices from abroad gained increasing influence, and many practitioners explored models of working that rejected the old-guard notion of the director as the person who simply 'explained' the text to the actors and issued a set of instructions on how it should be delivered.

The directors interviewed for this book were either part of the artistic revolution in the 1960s or have been powerfully influenced by it. Jatinder Verma, Ewan Marshall and Peter Cheeseman form part of a generation of pioneers in theatre, who have built up companies that speak with voices never before heard on stage in Britain. Lloyd Newson is a leading exponent of dance theatre, a form which is relatively new to British audiences. John Fox, Clifford McLucas and Mike Pearson have consistently challenged orthodox forms and sites of performance, seeking always to bring a wide range of disciplines to their work. Jonathan Miller and Declan Donnellan have experimented with classical texts and brought a visual inventiveness to traditional theatre, while Pete Brooks, Tim

Etchells, David Glass, Simon McBurney, Gerry Mulgrew and Ian Spink have experimented predominantly with physical and textual aspects of theatre and have insisted on a place for non-verbal as well as verbal narratives in their directing work. A significant element of the 1960s revolution has been the proliferation of women directors who have fought for space in what is still a male-dominated profession. Annie Castledine, for example, has defined herself as an outstanding director of European classical and contemporary plays, bringing a compelling visionary power to the stage. Likewise, Deborah Warner has created controversy with her challenging interpretations of classical plays and her experiments with gender and role play. Phyllida Lloyd and Katie Mitchell have broadened our knowledge of both classical and contemporary plays in fringe and mainstream theatre; Julia Pascal's work is an intriguing mix of multilingual poetics and the language of the body; and Garry Hynes brings an exciting vitality to new Irish plays. All these interviews demonstrate that there is not, and never has been, a universal way in which to understand process and practice, nor is there a universal way in which to understand the role of the director. Indeed, even the very word 'director' is associated with historical inflections which can be misleading and unhelpful.

Theatre and performance practices in 1990s Britain reveal the spread and co-existence of a multiplicity of approaches to 'directing', which David Glass defines in its widest sense as the organization of time, space and bodies of performers. Many of these directing approaches, however, have received little attention and have been scantily and erratically documented over the years. Some of the directors in this book may, therefore, not be known to you, and some would be viewed as 'new' by the mainstream, but they are established professionals in their field whose work challenges existing critical vocabularies.

Another reason for the scarcity of material on directors and directing practices in Britain must be the absence here of both oral and written traditions in the articulation of process. Ensemble work is common in continental Europe where the collaborative processes of theatre and performance are understood to underpin productions; dramaturgs act as the consciousness of process; critics and theatre analysts have historically sought to ask much broader intellectual questions about practice than we have been accustomed to in Britain. Consequently, the British still tend to perceive the director as a creative god, and the work of individual directors has been the subject of mystification, deemed to be beyond our understanding. It is extremely difficult for anyone to theorize the creative processes pertaining to a particular performance; terminologies seem inadequate and the so-called mysteries can be hard to fathom. Nonetheless, there is still much that can be expressed and understood. Romantic myths of impenetrable sublimity have given way to ideological inquiry, and the omnicreative director exists no more than the omniscient narrator.

It is this commitment to the articulation of what it is to be a director which the practitioners in this book share. Each director interviewed in this book gave a great deal of their time to thinking through their responses to our questions, and asked questions of themselves when they felt it was necessary. All the directors interviewed were involved in any rewriting or restructuring needed to clarify their thoughts at every stage of the editing process.

This book scratches the surface of a subject which urgently needs attention. We hope many more books will follow, thus celebrating the diversity of directing approaches which this book can only signal.

Gabriella Giannachi and Mary Luckhurst
Lancaster and Cambridge, July 1997

PETE BROOKS

Pete Brooks, who was born in Northern Ireland, is a writer and director. He studied English at Leeds University; after spending a year in France, he wrote an MA dissertation on Doris Lessing and the French existentialist novel at Leeds University. In the same year (1978) he was awarded the Buzz Goodbody Award for directing Barrie Keefe's *Abide With Me*. In 1979 he co-founded Impact Theatre Co-op. Impact toured nationally and internationally until 1986. From 1986 to 1992 he was a full-time lecturer in Theatre Studies at the universities of Lancaster and Manchester. During that time he formed Insomniac Productions and directed a number of highly successful and influential shows, including *Utopia* (1988), *L'Ascensore* (1992), *Woyzeck* (1993), *Claire de Luz* (1993), *Peepshow* (Paper Boat Award, Glasgow Mayfest, 1997), *Carnivali* (1998) and *Natura Muerta con Insectos* (Santiago de Chile, 1999). In 1993 he abandoned academic teaching and concentrated full-time on creative projects. He now divides his time between Insomniac Productions and freelance work, and is currently developing a number of film projects. He lives in London and spends much of his time in Chile.

What is your starting-point when making theatre?
I begin with an idea or a theme that I want to explore, usually something that I've had in my mind for years. Then there is a secondary starting-point, which is some kind of crystallizing idea, perhaps a narrative, or the idea for a character as performed by a particular actor, or an idea about staging. *Still Life with Insects* (1991), for example, was a narrative play that contained an idea I wanted to investigate. The situation was that two characters, twins, had been lied to by their father as a philosophical exercise. I'm fascinated by the idea of deliberately misleading an audience; in this piece I was also looking at the difficulties for all of us in negotiating a postmodern reality.

In *L'Ascensore* (1992), *Claire de Luz* (1993) and *Sangre* (1995), which were performance pieces, I was interested in their workings in relation to the gaze of the audience. I was playing with illusion in a filmic sense; I have a theory that as soon as we see an image framed cinematically we immediately think we will be entertained. One of my most insightful experiences lately was a production of *Claire de Luz* at the Riverside Festival in Stockton-on-Tees. This festival is for street theatre and *Claire de Luz* is really an art piece, languid and poetic, and I was warned that the audience was not accustomed to seeing work like this. In fact it was a great success and I think this was because of its framing; the way the shape of the frame could change and move. The audience felt as though they were watching a false film; they were used to film as a medium and felt they could understand it. Film is something people of all classes are familiar with and this is not true of theatre, which is still élitist and, I regret to say, a form that isn't necessarily associated with pleasure. I think if the audience had seen the piece on a stage in a theatre building they wouldn't have had the same relationship with it and perhaps wouldn't have enjoyed it.

How do you work in the rehearsal room?
Before I even reach the rehearsal room I have developed a close creative partnership with my designer. There are two designers who I've mainly worked with: Simon Vincenzi and Laura Hopkins. I develop the whole vocabulary of the piece with the designer and think out how the text, music, colours and staging work. I have a very strong sense of the language of a piece before I begin working with the actors.

What happens in the rehearsal room depends on the show. Unlike many other practitioners I don't have a strong methodology because one show is often quite different from another. I made a piece based on Georg Büchner's *Woyzeck* called *A Cursed Place* (1993), which was almost hyper-real in its appearance. I spent many hours in the rehearsals working on the characters and their interaction with each other in a conventional way, though the piece itself was not conventional. I am most concerned with the overall concept of a piece. So the lighting designer is just as important as the actors; by that I mean that the actors are simply *part* of a performance.

I think I probably work far more like a film director than a theatre director. To be honest, if directors cast well they should be able to solve a lot of their problems. If you work with a group of actors who are more or less an ensemble you can give them freedom and then edit what they do. I worked like this with Impact Theatre Company and now with Insomniac Productions.

Sometimes I have an incredibly specific idea of, say, a two minute sequence in a piece; I'll know because of a sense of rhythm akin to music. In other sections I'll think there are a number of alternatives and what matters is that the actors are comfortable with what they are doing. I remember a story someone once told me about Pina Bausch. She allegedly rehearsed a woman relentlessly for three days, saying only: 'Do it again.' The woman's sequence involved a rail of clothes, and at the end of this period the woman broke down, began to scream and shout and hurl all the clothes on the floor. At that point Pina said: 'That's perfect!' It's an apocryphal story and it paints an ambiguous picture of a director.

My background in devising meant that I didn't go into a rehearsal room with a script. I'm changing that now and going in with a more complete script; I'm more interested in writing than I used to be. Improvisation has always been part of the process of making theatre for me. There is also a great deal of discussion, and I'll talk myself out of a corner with the actors. In an ensemble you have to conceive of the show as fully as possible between yourselves; once everyone has understood what is required the piece has to be realized together. The real problem with devised work is that you don't reach the realization of a piece until a very late stage – if ever. There isn't the time for reflection or redrafting. Once everyone has the show in their heads, staging it is not immensely difficult; the problems come when there are holes in the thinking. Ideally I would like the following: a primary stage of imagining the piece through writing; a second stage of imagining the piece with actors; and a third stage of rehearsal and reflection. At present the middle stage is the part where everything happens, and I'm trying to change this by doing more work at the first stage and finding more time at the third stage.

Could you talk about this language of theatre that you develop before rehearsals?
I mean the development of a language which enables the articulation of a particular show. I think it's more obvious in relation to film: the way a film is designed affects how the characters in it can and can't speak. Films such as *Eraserhead* and *Bladerunner* are genre-based and the language has to reflect this. I start to imagine a conglomerate language to do with the way people sound and look. I'm fascinated by what I call the grammar of a piece: I often can't articulate my ideas until the language is right. The best film and theatre directors understand this instinctively.

What does the term 'director' mean to you?
I make theatre because I want to see my own visions on stage. I am the primary artist within that process and I've always seen myself as an 'artist' rather than anything else. I often wish I could be interested in making Shakespeare come alive, which I think is necessary and valuable, but I've found myself on the margins of the art form as a result of different interests.

There is an insecurity in theatre which I've heard expressed in the question: as a director are you an artist or technician? Nobody knows quite what they are. Many actors, for example, want to believe that they are highly trained professionals, but the best actors I've ever worked with have been natural talents. I find this debate about director training alarming. We have to ask ourselves *why* train a director. In my opinion the best way for a director to learn is to be given as many opportunities as possible to work with practitioners from diverse backgrounds.

How do you differentiate yourself from other practitioners?
I see myself as very much within a modernist tradition, which in British theatre is still fairly underground. I feel connected to the development of drama and I read and watch classical and contemporary theatre. Contemporary British theatre writing bores me in the main. I'd rather watch productions such as Stephen Daldry's *Machinal*, and consider how they were made. There is some great theatre in Britain, but there is also an overwhelming mediocrity.

Who and what influence you?
If I have to name the work that has most influenced me or encouraged me to believe that theatre is still a vital art form it would be Peter Brook's *A Midsummer Night's Dream*. Pip Simmon's *An die Musik*, The People Show, Pina Bausch's *1980* and Forced Entertainment's *200% & Bloody Thirsty* were all very important to me. I liked Steven Berkoff's work in the 1970s. I look to the European and American avant-garde, at artists such as Pina Bausch, Robert Wilson and Jan Fabre. I'd say my work has been innovative but not 'new' – it is certainly eclectic in its reference points. There is a dominance of theatre expounding a postmodern voice now. I find Forced Entertainment's work eloquent and moving but the sheer number of individuals cloning them fills me with despair. I developed my position within a plurality of voices during and after my student days in Leeds. I think that novel and film have influenced my work more directly than other theatre work.

What are your thoughts on audience?
I want to make work that is popular without being populist. Art is about pleasure, whether sensual, intellectual or paradoxically through the pain of emotional identification and catharsis. I think there are many ways of communicating with less sophisticated audiences. On the continent I've done a great deal of work that has played to audiences which cross all barriers of age and class. In Italy entire families go to my shows. Britain

has a snobbish resistance to the avant-garde that is not true of the rest of Europe, where the avant-garde is perceived as an inspiring galvanizer of mainstream theatre. In Britain we reduce shows to this derogatory term 'fringe', which seems to assume that what we all really want to do is have a West End hit.

I want to make work which draws in an audience from varied backgrounds. I wonder whether the future lies in street theatre, in events such as the Riverside Festival.

Are there certain themes and preoccupations running through your work?
More a series of questions, I think. Who are we? How do we make sense of ourselves? How do we deal with being alone? With death? I've always been concerned with the relationship between theory and practice. We live in a world which is visceral and present, yet the theorists describe it to us in ways which are more and more elusive and fractured. What do we do about that gulf?

I feel caught up in the death-throes of our culture. Since the collapse of the Soviet bloc we've been watching the death of capitalism – it's thrilling and romantic in some ways, no one knows what will happen. I often feel that the twentieth century happened between 1914 and 1962 and that those of us born after the Second World War have missed it. I romanticize, but the most significant thing in our generation has been the collapse of the Berlin Wall; to have been part of Gertrude Stein's lost generation, to have fought in the Spanish Civil War, this was the generation that *saw* the twentieth century. I was sixteen when I saw Neil Armstrong land on the moon and that was supposed to be the dawn of a new era. It wasn't. When we think of World War Two we think of the received mythology of a war fought against evil, but our impression of Vietnam is of a government that didn't know what it was doing and the consequent destruction of countless people. Our generation's experience is one of chaos.

How does this concern with history feed into your theatre work?
I become more and more interested in narrative. Stories are much more complex than I used to think. In the early eighties, confessing an interest in narrative was rather like confessing that you read pornography! Now I feel that there's so much chaos that we need stories; we need their structures in order to be able to get a glimpse at things. Many practitioners and university lecturers want to be 'postmodern postmodernists', and they legitimate poor performance work in the name of

LIVERPOOL JOHN MOORES UNIVERSITY
LEARNING SERVICES

modern theoretical, post-quantum chaos. In the end you have to take a position; too many use the theories of postmodernism in order to avoid taking a position. There is a new orthodoxy abroad in the universities. The new theory is sexy and beguiling. I have taught in places where performances are called 'statements in action' – personally I prefer the word 'show'. I did a postgraduate degree and spent seven years teaching theatre; I left because I was meant to be teaching contemporary practice and I felt that I was losing touch with theatre altogether.

Where do you position yourself now?
I feel more and more on my own. In the last few years I've spent a lot of time in South America, South East Asia and Australia, so I feel less Eurocentric and I'm not interested in 'the scene'. I work best when I make work without thinking about what others are doing. I don't want to be seduced into changing my work for the benefit of funding bodies. One can be too easily influenced. Something like the National Revue of Live Art, for example, is a good thing, but it also helps to create an orthodoxy of its own, particularly in the institutions of higher education. I know, I've taught in them and seen it happening.

How would you like to develop your work?
My dream is to build a forty-nine seater construction which I could take on tour. The seating would be in rows of seven by seven and inside everything would be completely controlled by computers and projectors. I would make detailed, dark narratives. This is purely for myself, for research purposes. I was working some way towards this with *Claire de Luz*, for which we constructed a miniature cinema.

I'm not sure what the future is for Insomniac at the moment. I've become increasingly disillusioned with the endless compromises one makes in the name of funding, and there are many pressures and problems. I do a mixture of teaching and freelance work as well, and I look to develop the freelance angles.

I find it difficult to get excited about a show containing just three or four people now. I made a piece called *The Girl* (1990) at Lancaster University with thirty students; it's impossible to reproduce this in professional theatre.

In the next couple of years I'm determined to make a couple of independent short films. I'm disappointed by a great deal of theatre. I love it, but I am beginning not to like its transience; as I get older I want to do something fixed. The movies are available historically.

ANNIE CASTLEDINE

Born near Rotherham, South Yorkshire, Annie Castledine trained as a lecturer in Theatre Studies. Her early career was spent at Bulmershe College which is now part of the University of Reading. She became the Arts Council trainee director at the Theatre Royal York in 1979, after which she started working as a professional theatre director. While she was in York, she formed her own theatre company, Northern Studio Theatre, which was dedicated to the development of new writing in the north of England. Subsequently, Castledine was Associate Artistic Director of Theatr Clwyd from 1985 to 1987, and Artistic Director of Derby Playhouse from 1987 to 1990. It was during this time that she defined herself as a visionary and innovative director with a special affinity for plays by female playwrights. Among her most notable productions from this period are: Lillian Hellman's *The Children's Hour* (1987), Mary Pix's *The Innocent Mistress* (1987), Gerlind Reinshagen's *Sunday's Children* (1988) and Lucy Gannon's *Wicked Old Nellie* (1989). Castledine also co-produced and co-directed a number of projects, including Molière's *The School for Wives*, co-directed with Neil Bartlett (1990), and Marie Luise Fleisser's *Pioneers in Ingolstadt* and *Purgatory in Ingolstadt*, co-directed with Stephen Daldry (1991). Since 1990 she has been working freelance. She has also edited volumes 9 and 10 of the Methuen series *Plays by Women*. She was awarded the Bass Charrington London Fringe Award for Best Director (1989–90) and the Time Out Award for Best Director (1991). The Derby Playhouse was nominated for the Prudential Award for Theatre (1989). Her freelance work has enabled her to be involved with Theatre de Complicite and laboratory work within the Royal National Theatre Studio. She has also experimented with the form of the one-person theatre piece, notably *Goliath* (1996) and *Hymn to Love* (1998).

How would you define theatre?
Theatre is a made thing, an artifice highly wrought. It is not prey to the spontaneous or the haphazard irrationality of real life. Through theatre we explore the instability of every circumstance. Theatre is a highly collaborative art which requires much of everyone and is full of risk. The art of theatre contributes to our understanding of the greatest art of all – the art of living. If I had to choose one piece of theatre which offers a

definition of theatre at its simplest I would choose Claire Coulter's performance of *The Fever* by Wallace Shawn (1996–7), which represents a woman on a bentwood chair delivering a complex verbal text with the most minimal physical text; the performer transported us, engaged us, provoked us, moved us and, most of all, made us think and change. Theatre should be constantly open, never closed. It should be always changing and adapting in order to survive. It should incite and communicate ideas which engage and fill us with wonder. It should be sensuous and full of tension. It should be about dreams.

What is a director?

A director is like a messenger whose message is too accurate, truthful and well realized – in other words, a person everyone should want to shoot. A director is also a visionary, someone who is not afraid to present the times as they see them. A director is responsible for the quality of life of everyone involved in a piece that they're directing, and is aware that the process of making theatre is also about how to live and about the sharing of values and ideals which should inform every rehearsal. Ultimately, a director is a child who can enable the performers to recover childhood at will and who understands the importance of play.

What are your preoccupations as a director?

At the moment I have two concerns: how to make classic text by writers such as Shakespeare, Ibsen, Brecht, Sophocles, Williams and O'Neill speak for a modern audience; and making sure that the work of twentieth-century women writers such as Marguerite Duras, Claire Luckham, Maureen Lawrence, Elfriede Jelinek, Lina Wertmuller, Marie Luise Fleisser and Gerlind Reinshagen is known and understood. I am fascinated with texts which are innovatory in form and define our theatre vocabulary. My production with Annabel Arden of Duras's *India Song* (1993) and my recent workshop at the Royal National Theatre Studio of Gerlind Reinshagen's *The Green Door* (1996), as well as the adaptation from J. M. Coetzee's novel *Foe*, co-directed with Marcello Magni for Theatre de Complicite (1996), are all examples of these concerns. I am a socialist and so I am obsessed with presenting voices which are not often heard: the voices of the inarticulate, the dispossessed and the disenfranchised. My productions of Endesha Ida Mae Holland's *From the Mississippi Delta* (1989 and 1993), Maureen Lawrence's *Tokens of Affection* (1990), Sheila Yeger's *Self Portrait* (1990), Biyi Bandele Thomas's *Marching for Fausa* (1993) and my production of Bryony Lavery's *Goliath* are all driven by my politics.

Another of my major preoccupations is the politics of collaboration. A production that revealed both of these preoccupations was Angela Fisher's *Brecht's Women* (1978), which was an exploration of collaboration and an investigation into the qualities of stillness. This production could serve as a metaphor for the continuous and abiding themes of my work. The text examined Brecht's relationship with Elizabeth Hauptmann, Marguerite Steffin, Ruth Berlau and Helene Weigel, and challenged the notion of Brecht's authorship. It was a devised piece developed through extensive research and improvisation with the writer always present in rehearsal. Music played a large part (the musical director was Andy Dodgson) and the piece was thought to be so provocative by the Brecht estate that it had an injunction slapped upon it and we were forced to play it underground.

These days I spend a lot of time with young directors from whom I learn an enormous amount. Being in dialogue with my contemporaries is something about which I am passionate. I believe in the free exchange of ideas and give a lot of my time to discussion. The most important thing for me in such a product- and market-driven society is giving theatrical form to my dreams about how society could be. These dreams must surface in my work. They are the motor that drives it.

What is your principal medium?
Physical text and verbal text. By physical text I mean every action occurring through the body of the performer. In my early work especially, my interest in physical text involved looking at stillness. For instance, I was interested in understanding the role of 'natural stillness' and I explored the difference between choreographed and non-choreographed gesture. I believe that performers have to go through a long journey to find the position of stillness from which they can do everything while seeming to do nothing. I think that every movement, every gesture has to carry a line of meaning. No movement should be unchoreographed.

I delight in exploring form and structure and tend towards making pieces of theatre that use my compositional skills of devising, improvising and adapting. I also spend a lot of time thinking and working on the aesthetics of the live body on stage; how we move, speak and dress. In my opinion the politics of the body has been underexplored. I want to create invigorating and essential theatre which excites the senses and portrays my dreams about society. This is why I am obsessed with aesthetics. I think that everything in a piece of theatre has to be harmonious. Even a postmodern and disjunctive performance has to be structured.

What is the guiding principle of your directing practice?
A knowledge of ambiguity. A realization that things are never finished. There is always a mystery and there can be no mystery if things finish.

I always work with the whole ensemble for the entire duration of the rehearsal time. I want to enable performers to look for the characters they will be representing from within themselves. Where do they look? How do they look? How do they bring out their own devils without being afraid of finding the character? I use improvisation, music, dance, film, close textual analysis or deconstruction of the text, whatever means I can to help the performers to find resemblances in their own lives to the characters they are playing. Texts shouldn't pass through the performers like strange or foreign objects: performers should be absolutely and entirely conscious of everything that they do, so that they can be in absolute control of what they do. This is why I also try to develop within each performer a critical attitude and an awareness of how our contemporary society is working. Everything I do as a director must enable the performer's consciousness to be at its most heightened level.

For instance, the performers I worked with in Jelinek's *What Happened after Nora Left her Husband* (1996) were initially quite removed from the text and found it difficult to work with the original German and the translation, both of which were highly stylized. They also found it difficult to assimilate the text's analysis of Marxism and capitalism and its references to Ibsen's *A Doll's House* and *Pillars of Society*. Moreover, the text was set in a textile factory. What did the performers know of Germany in 1922? What did they know about working in a textile factory? As a director I had to encourage them to research these issues in order to familiarize themselves with all aspects of the text. Before allocating roles, we looked at *A Doll's House* and Jelinek's text together so that the ensemble could deepen their knowledge of Jelinek's source. I did this by arranging for a choreographed physical reading in sequence, working in the space, rather than around the table. I also organized a visit to a textile factory, viewings of films, political debates on Marxism and capitalism and did improvisations which included lots of physical work so the performers could begin to understand the piece and at the same time bond together as an ensemble. But this is only one example of the way I work. Rehearsals cannot be defined and, most of all, they cannot be repeated. Rehearsals depend on the needs of the text and the needs of the ensemble which vary from situation to situation.

Has your notion of directing changed over the years?
Yes, it certainly has. I am reminded that when someone met Brecht
after a ten-year gap and said with enthusiasm, 'How lovely to see you.
You haven't changed at all!', Brecht's face lost all its colour and became
quite grey.

I have become much more interested in co-directing. My first experience of co-directing was with Stephen Daldry at The Gate Theatre in
1991 when we worked on *Pioneers in Ingolstadt* and *Purgatory in Ingolstadt*
by Fleisser. We challenged, empowered and questioned – but never
threatened – each other in creating what I felt was a very innovatory piece
of theatre. My collaboration with Theatre de Complicite began in 1992
with the production of *The Winter's Tale* and has continued with *The
Three Lives of Lucie Cabrol* (1994), *Out of a House Walked a Man* (1994), *Foe*
(1996) and *The Caucasian Chalk Circle* (1997). This way of directing has
enabled me to change, develop, share, listen and be inspired.

Who and what have acted as influences on your work?
Brecht, Shakespeare, Ibsen and a wide range of European women playwrights. The writings of Stanislavski, Edward Gordon Craig, Augusto
Boal and the work of Joan Littlewood were all influences on my early
life. The performers and collaborators with whom I have worked during the earlier part of my career in Theatr Clwyd and the Derby Playhouse were also formative influences. Designers such as Martin Johns,
Anthony Ward, Ian McNeil, Ruari Murchison, Jennie Blincow, Andy
Miller and Bill Pinner have had a great impact on my work, and composers such as Adrian Johnson, Peter Heyward and Juwon Ogumbe, as
well as musicians such as Anna Hemery and Helen Glavin, have enabled
me to realize my constant desire to have live music as part of any piece
of theatre. My most recent work has been in television, and I feel that
this is going to be an enormous influence on my work in the future.

How do you see yourself in terms of the European theatrical landscape?
I am part of this landscape and I have directed work of writers from
almost every country in Europe. I travel to see the work of my European colleagues as often as possible. My one regret is that I cannot work
with them in this country as often as I would like.

Do you feel that you can work as you want to work in this country?
The short answer is no. I want a lot more preparation time, rehearsal

time, training time and infinitely more funding than is considered worthy in this country. Theatre is an abused art form here, and it is undervalued because it is under-funded. The English still regard theatre as something to do with childlike amateurs who are regarded with amused toleration whilst everyone waits for them to grow up. Deep within the English psyche there is still that Puritan distrust of theatre makers. Sadly, I also think that it is still true that the voices of women playwrights are marginalized.

What would you hope to see developing in terms of the director in the future?
In a poem called 'On the Critical Attitude' (1938) Brecht wrote that the education of a person or the transformation of a state are instances both of fruitful criticism and of art. This poem means a lot to me because I think that theatre is a life-changing medium which can affect our views, change our attitudes, counter prejudice, revitalize and civilize our minds, and expand and enrich our understanding of life. Theatre should be as much a part of life as oxygen or water. Theatre links with the very first response we have to the universe: the desire to play. This desire to make theatre stays with us all our lives, but some people feel removed from it because it is so expensive. I would like theatre to be highly subsidized so that it could be available to everybody. Only then can we argue that we are developing a better society.

Peter Cheeseman

Born in Portsmouth in 1932, Peter Cheeseman graduated from Sheffield University in 1959 with an Arts degree and a Teaching diploma. He started working in the professional theatre as Assistant Director of Derby Playhouse in 1959 and joined Stephen Joseph's theatre in the round company in 1961. He was Director of the Victoria Theatre in Stoke-on-Trent from 1962 to 1984, when he and his company moved to the New Victoria Theatre in the neighbouring town of Newcastle-under-Lyme. He directed classics, including plays by Sophocles, Plautus, Shakespeare, Molière, Ibsen, Brecht and Anouilh, and contemporary playwrights such as Alan Ayckbourn, Peter Whelan, Peter Terson, Nick Darke, Shane Connaughton and Arthur Berry. Cheeseman is best known for the creation of eleven musical documentaries, on which he worked with and for the local community of Stoke-on-Trent and Newcastle-under-Lyme. In recognition of his achievements he was awarded Honorary Degrees by the Universities of Keele (1967), Wolverhampton (1992) and Staffordshire (1998), and appointed a C.B.E. in the 1998 New Year's Honours List. He retired from the Directorship of the New Victoria Theatre in January 1998 to write a book about his work and enjoy freelance directing. He now also serves as Chairman of the National Council for Drama Training.

What is your principal medium?
Theatre and, specifically, theatre in the round. I began, as most people did, in what might be described as mono-directional theatre, then I started working in Stephen Joseph's theatre and have been working in the round ever since. I am not only a theatre director, but the director of a theatre, and I have chosen to be the director of a theatre in the round.

What is the importance of theatre in the round for you?
When I was a student I felt very frustrated about the remoteness of the actors, particularly since in those days students often worked in halls with flat floors and raised stages like an English school hall. In this context the sense of remoteness of the actor was considerable, whereas I wanted the audience to be much closer. When the spotlight made footlights redundant and apron stages began to be used, everybody in the theatre started to look at the relationship with the audience in a differ-

ent way; and when cinema and television took up the pictorial role of theatre, and theatre had to find its own destiny once again, most of us wanted to make the actor more important and not just part of a stage picture.

Most of these innovations happened in the fifties and sixties. I remember this coming to a climax for me in a production of Shelagh Delaney's *A Taste of Honey* at Derby Playhouse, when one of the actresses came right down on to the forestage and leaned against the proscenium arch. This actress was really in touch with the audience in a way one could never be from *behind* the proscenium arch. It was a moment of illumination and I realized that this was the quality I wanted to work with. Then I was offered a job by Stephen Joseph, the great protagonist of the theatre in the round. His vision of the spatial relationship between the actor and the audience and his way of radically appraising the importance of its components fascinated me. I had never met anybody who had such a clear, radical vision of the essential importance of the physical structure of theatre. This vision affected me and Alan Ayckbourn for the rest of our working lives. We both realized that the potency of this medium was limitless.

How did you feel when you first directed something in the round?
Stephen gave me some words of advice: he said that theatre in the round is structured like life, and that consequently movement organizes itself like it does in real life. In the proscenium theatre one spends a lot of time organizing movement, whereas in the theatre in the round there is virtually a limitless possibility for the actor to move at any one time. In the circle everybody is equal and everybody has equal access to each other. So when I first directed a production in the round I felt a tremendous sense of freedom.

How did you first come across documentary theatre?
Through film and television, especially during the war when documentaries were very important. When I was a teenager in Liverpool, there was a left-wing group called Unity Theatre which had put on some Living Newspaper performances. I was very struck by the flavour of it. Other major influences were the documentary theatres of Piscator and Brecht. When I first became director of the Victoria Theatre in the sixties it seemed that documentary theatre productions were the solution to a number of problems I had at the time. Stephen Joseph had always encouraged writers to work with the company. The only one left in the

acting company when we settled at the old Victoria Theatre was Alan Ayckbourn, and when Alan moved in 1964 we had no writer on our staff. I believed that the presence of a writer in the company was particularly important for actors in respecting the skill involved in writing a play, so for me losing the writer was terribly dangerous. I was also interested in the creative potencies of the group and in the potency of collaborative work: tuning myself into the world around me became very important and it seemed to me that the company could do this collectively. This was the time when creating text from improvisation was fashionable. I wasn't just interested in making up plays, I also wanted to create material out of the community. So I thought that we could explore the life and history of the community by creating the material ourselves. I think that it's all very well to be related to the community, but I believe that the community has to be on stage at some point in time. Yet very quickly I found that I got more and more unhappy about making things up, about improvising. Then Charles Parker introduced me to the notion of using contemporary material by recording it on tape. He just said to me, 'Listen! Listen to people talking!'

What is the rehearsal process you adopt when you do documentary theatre?
It is a preparatory process that then becomes a rehearsal process. When I began in 1964, my notion was that this preparatory process had to be done by the actors. For my first documentary show, *The Jolly Potters* (1964), which was about the industrial conditions in the Potteries in the 1840s, I had done a bit of research on my own, but the script only started to be created by the actors when they came into rehearsal. I used improvisation in combination with edited primary source material with *The Jolly Potters* and *The Staffordshire Rebels* (1965), which was about the English Civil War and its effects on the people of Staffordshire.

I gradually evolved a rehearsal process over the years. By the production of *Fight for Shelton Bar!* (1974) I had changed my way of working quite substantially. *Fight for Shelton Bar!* was about the struggle by Shelton steelworkers and their families to stop the closure of the plant. It was composed almost exclusively of transcribed tape-recorded material. My system of work was this. Up to several months' initial research was done by me and (if we had one at the time) the resident writer, or by one or two members of the permanent acting company who were free of rehearsals. At a later stage even more members of the company would join in. The play in rehearsal just before the documentary was a small-cast play which enabled half of the permanent company, which consisted of thirteen or fourteen actors, to join in. This process normally took a month. During this phase we went out tape recording final interviews in the community and discussed them collectively. At that stage we only had a basic notion of a storyline. It is impossible to handle the material from tape recordings until it is turned into some form of writing. It could involve dozens of tapes! So this phase was very important to us. By the time the rehearsals began we already had a structure, but we didn't have scenes. At this stage the entire company, and some of the interviewees whose stories were being told, started meeting in the rehearsal room. Rehearsals consisted in turning this material into scenes and creating songs. At that point a lot of detail was added to the stories and the actors were often shown by the interviewees what exactly had happened to them. Finally the songs were added, often fulfilling a narrative function and linking various scenes together.

This format has been modified over the years. Now we no longer have the kind of permanent company we had in the sixties and seventies. So for *The Dirty Hill*, the first documentary in the new theatre in 1990, I had to do all the work with my Associate Director, Rob Swain. In *Nice Girls* (1993), the story of three women who occupied Trentham Colliery in 1993, the women about whom the story centred came into the rehearsal room and improvised everything that had happened to them. We just recorded it and the actresses watched them. That was extraordinary and had never happened before.

What are the guiding principles of your directing practice?
Giving a community an identity, its historical identity, through retelling its stories on the stage is at the heart of my work. In all productions what I create is a composite work of art, made by a group of people, and the most important thing about each production is its uniqueness. My guiding principle is to help in achieving the best we can do as a particular group of people working on a specific production at a particular point in time. This also informs my work as a director of a theatre. Here I believe my most important responsibility is the organization of an environment sympathetic to the creative processes involved in making theatre.

I am not a director who likes to have strong concepts and I have always been nervous and antipathetic about themed ways of looking at productions. I suppose that I am very puritanical in terms of my approach to the text. I believe in working exclusively from the text, rather than bringing outside influences to it. Looking at my role as a creator of text, my priorities are more political and socially conscious, and they are very much related to my role in this community. In this light it becomes very important for me to tell the stories of the community. This has been my great mission. As a director of a theatre it is also very important for me to make the richness of dramatic texts available to the whole community. The most important formative experience I had in my life was when I was an officer in the Royal Air Force. I joined their Education Branch and did a lot of teaching. At some point I was teaching English literature to three non-commissioned officers on the brink of leaving the service. They had no literary background and I loved the idea of lighting a flame of passion for words in them. Not everybody is so lucky to get an education, or to have an inspiring teacher or access to a theatre, and so to be able to give something to people of the richness of language, of words, became the most important thing in my life.

Another principle for me is that I have to put myself in the place of the audience – as a director I have to be representative of them. I feel obsessively that actors should have a sense of integrity, of not pretending, so that what they do is as real and true as possible. In theatre in the round an audience can see into the back of an actor's head, so if the actor tells lies, the audience spots it immediately. I think actors should be in direct contact with the audience and this is why documentary is important to me. In the kind of documentary theatre I do the actor does not pretend to become another person, he or she becomes the advocate for that person. The actors address the audiences themselves, saying: 'I am not this person, I am speaking for this person.' This openness and sincerity are encouraged by theatre in the round. The difference between theatre and television, of course, is that theatre is live. In this sense theatre celebrates the presence of the actor and there is no room for any deception. In documentary theatre there needs to be considerable restraint and a certain objectivity in the playing of each part.

Do you think there is such thing as a universal performance language?
I suppose so. Probably some kind of mime. However, I am not particularly interested in it. I work with specificity. Universal languages don't appeal to me. Even in a multi-cultural or multi-ethnic production, what is interesting to me is the specificity of each culture, of each ethnic group: what interests me in documentary theatre is the celebration of difference.

How does awareness of audience affect your work?
In a number of ways. Apart from the ways I have described already, the fact that the audience is so present in theatre in the round means that my obsession is meeting the imaginative potential of this situation. Stephen Joseph said that theatre is made of actors and audiences: their interrelationship is what is important to me.

Another issue is that the kind of audiences who come to my theatre in Stoke-on-Trent are not necessarily intellectually sophisticated, and so I always try to break down barriers and prejudices. Accents, for instance, are a problem: if you speak with a southern accent, you are often mistaken here in North Staffordshire for an upper-class person. Moreover, people here are much more old-fashioned in terms of their morality and one has to be careful not to offend them. With students and young people I am also aware that what they see here might be the only experience they ever have in the theatre.

How would you describe theatre in a simple way?
I would say that it's a way of telling a story in which everyone in the story pretends to be one of the people in the story. I think theatre is a sophisticated way of telling stories. I think these days we are in danger of underestimating the enormous complexity and richness of words.

How do you see yourself in terms of the European theatrical landscape?
As an unknown British regional theatre director.

Do you feel that you can work as you like in this country?
I think that in terms of funding the situation is catastrophic. Many theatres are being forced to close. Even here, we are on the edge of impossibility. In order to keep the theatre dynamic one has to be able to take risks, and financially we can't afford to take risks. The situation for theatre in this country is becoming very serious indeed.

DECLAN DONNELLAN

Declan Donnellan was born in England of Irish parents. He read English at Cambridge University and was called to the bar. He co-founded Cheek by Jowl Theatre Company with Nick Ormerod in 1981. The rise of Cheek by Jowl was meteoric; the company has widened the British theatrical repertoire by giving British premières of *Andromache* (1984) by Jean Racine, *The Cid* (1986) by Pierre Corneille and *A Family Affair* (1988) by Aleksandr Ostrovsky. To date Cheek by Jowl has represented Britain at major arts festivals round the world and performed in five continents. Donnellan was an Associate Director of the Royal National Theatre from 1989–1998 and his productions there include: Lope de Vega's *Fuente Ovejuna* (1988), Henrik Ibsen's *Peer Gynt* (1990), Stephen Sondheim's *Sweeney Todd* (1993) and Tony Kushner's *Angels in America* (1992–3). He has directed the *School for Scandal* at the Royal Shakespeare Company, *Le Cid* for the Avignon Festival and *The Winter's Tale* for the Maly Drama Theatre of St Petersburg.

What is your starting-point as a director?
One of the aims of Cheek by Jowl is to re-examine the classic texts of world theatre and to investigate them in a fresh and unsentimental way, eschewing directorial concepts to focus on the actor and the actor's art. So I start by choosing a play and then I seek out actors. I have a system of reading the play repeatedly and forming ideas, not necessarily about the 'types' of people I want in it, but about the psychologies I sense to be at work in the text. Putting together a company for each play is a long process, and I will see actors several times, musing on the onstage dynamics between characters. Normally I assemble fourteen actors and aim for a seven-week rehearsal period.

How do you work in the rehearsal room?
I never start with a read-through. For the first few days I do everything other than the text! I might begin with exercises based on the world of the play, with singing and dancing. For *As You Like It* (1994) Sue Lefton worked on movement with the company, and we did exercises that revolved around gender and sex roles; everyone tried playing the opposite gender. At the same time I also had the idea of using tango as a

means of exploring the play; it's a very political dance about who is in control, which is a key question in the play. This is a rare example of an idea I had at the beginning of the rehearsal process that was actually worked into the performance. Most of my ideas at the start of rehearsal are not workable and are almost invariably ditched later on.

I don't 'see' the play in my head before I enter the rehearsal room, or indeed during the rehearsal process, and I may not like what I have done when the performance goes on. What I do is problem solve: when I begin the rehearsals I have the text and the actors, and I set myself the fiction that I'm not an interpreter and try to do the play as well as I can, working with the actors as well as I can. As far as possible I try to banish judgementalism from the rehearsal room, the sense that what the actor does is either right or wrong; this is difficult because all of us tend to seek approval for our actions. I stress to the company that what we are trying to do is perform a text as well as we can, and of course experience teaches you what 'well' may mean. I have had to ignore British traditions of acting Shakespeare; I would never claim that my work is 'original', but I do seek fresh insights for actors and aim to reassert the energy of Shakespeare's plays.

I always want the actors to know all their lines from the first day we work on the text, and I understand that I am unusual in this demand. I find it very difficult if actors do not know their lines. I have to hear and see a line from an actor without the book in their hand, otherwise I find I am distracted and unable to explore a line or a moment in any depth. I expect every actor to do a lot of research, not just on their part, but on the play, the time in which the play is set, the philosophy, the geography and anything that may be useful. The research is a useful tool for freeing the actor's imagination. I never conduct discussions with actors round a table; I never hold forth on the meaning of a play because a director is not the authority on the meanings of a play. There is talk, of course, but it is always within the context of rehearsal, in the context of actors moving in a space.

I have to say that for me there is no technique to directing a play. I never have any preconceived idea of how I will rehearse. That idea emerges once I have begun the process. The important thing is to know that you don't know how you will proceed. Every scene in a play presents its own problems, but suddenly and unexpectedly I see a surge of life in a particular moment and I go chasing after it. I do a multitude of exercises on the text, try many different approaches to a specific problem, but gradually I piece together the moments that are full of life. I often find that the resolution of a problem will come at a moment when there is no conscious attempt to unlock it: I might have been flogging a dead horse, so I call a halt, we all relax, and in that break I may catch an interesting gesture out of the corner of my eye, or hear an actor deliver a line in a way that gives me an idea.

What is a director?
Primarily, I see myself as someone who releases an actor's confidence in their ability to act, as someone who endeavours to stop actors from passing judgement on themselves. I am the coach and the actor is the athlete. The notion that a director creates 'rules' is notoriously problematic, but clearly I impose rules, though what I impose I see emerge from the grass-roots, from the actors themselves, and I choose to reimpose it on them at certain points. There should be very few rules in rehearsal. Rules are there to enable us to tell the truth: whenever we seem to be faced with a choice between telling the truth or obeying the rule, we should always choose to break the rule.

Your professional partnership with the designer Nick Ormerod is well known. How do you work together?
Nick is present throughout the rehearsal process because all decisions about design and costume evolve from the actors' performances. This way of working is central to the philosophy of Cheek by Jowl. There are no secret, magic meetings between Nick and me when we retire and decide on everything outside the rehearsal room. Sometimes there are difficulties: for example, when we work at the National Theatre, the design has to be submitted before rehearsals and there is no possibility of modification. We both find this constricting and I am never able to help Nick with the preparation of the model. I am not someone with a fascination for toy theatres, and I don't understand how to use models! My understanding of space derives from seeing actors move. In fact, we both make all our crucial discoveries through watching the actors: this is where the way we both work has most in common.

What are your thoughts on audience?
On average I go once a week to see Cheek by Jowl productions. As a director I try to set up a simple structure which gives room to the actors and allows for surprise. It is very important to me that the audiences for Cheek by Jowl are heterogeneous. This normally is the case, but in the past there have been occasions when I found out that all the tickets for a

performance had been sold to a specific group. On one strange occasion in Moscow the audience was entirely made up of schoolteachers.

I was taught much about theatre by my English teacher Philip Lawrence; he took me to see many plays and introduced me to Shakespeare. I vividly remember the Royal Shakespeare Company's seasons during the 1970s. As a schoolboy it was vital to me that I experienced going to the theatre as an intrusion into a glamorous and sophisticated adult world. These days Cheek by Jowl require that no more than 25 per cent of the audience will be made up of school parties: this is precisely because we are very concerned that theatre should be an exciting place for young people and not a destination for worthy school trips. It is important to draw young people to the theatre as individuals and not herd them along in packs 'for their own good'. I know that I condemned anything that I attended in school uniform as dull and reactionary. Cheek by Jowl has always striven to bring young audiences into the theatre, but that does not mean that theatre should simplify itself. What needs to be addressed is not the organization of mass theatre trips, but the question of how those responsible for theatre can stimulate and encourage young people to come to the theatre of their own accord.

Who and what have influenced your work as a director?
I have been profoundly influenced by Peter Brook, by his simplicity, showmanship and his humanity. I love his work for the way it always encompasses the poles of the spiritual and the vulgar. Is it more important to breathe or eat? – you have to do both but if you don't do either you'll die. I saw Brooks's *A Midsummer Night's Dream* when I was sixteen and have never forgotten it. I have also been influenced by dance companies: I saw a lot of ballet as a teenager. I used to take a tube from Ealing every Saturday and go to watch the Royal Shakespeare Company or buy cheap tickets for matinées at the Royal Court. I think human beings are influenced by what they enjoy.

I've always been fascinated by watching actors play scenes. I loathe mannered acting, and love Russian actors for the definition of their performance. Russian companies take the tradition of acting even more seriously than the British.

I've studied many visual artists and their work, and I am especially moved by the Spanish masters. Zurbaran, for example, painted a series of saints, which are very simple and represent each individual utterly absorbed in an action, rather than in an artificial pose for the spectator. I find self-absorption in an action enthralling and relate it to my love of watching actors. Rembrandt also fascinates me for his depiction of human movement entirely abandoned to the present moment, or for the detail of how someone stands. I'm drawn to work that contrasts form against background. I would never think of recreating pictures on stage, but paintings do inform my creativity.

What are your hopes for the future of theatre and for yourself?
I was recently at a conference in Pisa and heard many bewailing the death of theatre. My own feeling is that theatre will survive, despite our best attempts to kill it. As a live art form it is unique; those who succeed us will develop theatre in new, exciting ways. Ultimately theatre is an archetypal need. It will reassert itself from generation to generation without any need of tradition. One of the great privileges of touring Cheek by Jowl's work is that I have experienced plays in very different cultures. I am often asked about differences in reception, but actually what always strikes me are the similarities that remain, what we have in common with each other, what does not pass away. The human capacity for these cross-cultural moments of communal understanding fills me with wonder.

My response to theatre has not become more sophisticated over time. As a teenager I sat in the audience and desperately wanted to be part of the performance; now I've become part of the performance in a different way. This sense of belonging, or of wanting to belong, is fundamental to my understanding of live performance; playmaking is essentially a shared experience. I long to be a writer but I find it difficult to sit down and work in isolation. I think it is important not to lose sight of the tremendous creativity of actors, and to appreciate an actor for the precision of their craft. There is something both beautiful and healing about the collective creative process of theatre, and nothing is more crushing than watching a play which has been stifled of life.

Sometimes I am frustrated by the thought that theatre is ephemeral and that I will leave no trace behind me; on the other hand, it's also a liberating thought. Theatre is a place where we dream communally; it is not the result of one person's effort.

Where do you locate yourself as a director?
I entertain people by telling stories, and for me a crux of the director's work is deciding *what* the story is and *how* it should be told.

TIM ETCHELLS

Born in 1962, Tim Etchells graduated in English and Drama from Exeter University in 1984. In the same year he and a group of other artists founded Forced Entertainment in Sheffield. He has directed and written texts for each of the company's works since 1986; these include: *200% & Bloody Thirsty* (1987), *Marina & Lee* (1990), *Emanuelle Enchanted* (1992), *Speak Bitterness* (1995), *Quizooa!* (1997) and *Dirty Work* (1998). He has published a collection of short fiction, *Endland Stories* (Pulp Books, 1999), and a collection of performance texts with critical and theoretical writings titled *Certain Fragments* (Routledge, 1999).

How would you define theatre?
I think theatre is about going somewhere to watch something.

What is your principal medium?
I work with action, text, video, music, set – with more or less anything that can be placed in a performance arena. In different projects these elements combine or recombine, but we don't have an agenda about what has priority. *Speak Bitterness* (1995) is a performance that's almost entirely text-based, while *12 a.m. Awake & Looking Down* (1993) featured no text whatsoever. All we care about is that something is at stake.

We work through long improvisations, long explorations, and I think during this process I basically wait for something to happen – for something that implicates me, as an audience member, for a combination of things that somehow might constitute an event. I'm sitting in rehearsals and waiting for that moment when I lean forwards in the chair, or when my heart skips a beat, or when I think, 'That's incredible, that's scary.'

Could you elaborate on your notion of 'event'?
The performance artist Chris Burden described people who saw his work as witnesses rather than as spectators or audience members. He was making a distinction about one's implication in what happens, about the status of an event rather than of a performance. Events are real. When the performance takes on something of event-hood then it becomes interesting to me.

What are the guiding principles of your directing practice?

My guiding principle is to wait and see. This is why I take five, six months to direct a piece, though not necessarily in a row. We prefer rehearsing when we are miles away from the deadline – you can't experiment much when you are too close to the deadline because you are too nervous and can't spend much time on a new idea. I guess that my contribution to the piece as a director is to let things find their own place. For instance, Terry O'Connor was working with some text in *Hidden J* (1994–5); she would perform it like some bizarre erotic story, and I knew that there was something there, but for ages I couldn't quite work out what was happening. So in improvisations I let it happen and I let it happen, until one day it became clear to me what the text should be, what function it had in relation to the rest of the piece. Things find their own place – it's very important to me not to force arbitrary solutions. It's the difference between making a decision and arriving at one – I'm much more interested in the latter. Sometimes I think that my task as a director is to fix meanings, to nail things down and make them more precise, but I always want to do this without solidifying them too much, without taking out the gaps that the audience needs to elaborate on the piece.

Can you describe how you work on a piece from day one?

As a company, we will develop a list of things that we are vaguely interested in, such as a couple of fragments of text, an idea about space, some ideas about costume or action or whatever. Then from day one we'll begin to work with these things in combination, exploring them through improvisation, adding new ideas, mutating them. We usually build some crude environment in which to work, using materials from old sets or whatever else is to hand. The building of this environment is really important to us. We need a place to work. If you put us in an empty room we can't do anything.

Why?

Because our work is tied to objects and particular places and spaces. I feel that I haven't got any imagination at all unless I see things happening. In *Speak Bitterness* (1995), for instance, all the rehearsal work we did before raising the actors on the platform was almost a waste of time. It was only when they were raised from the floor that it made any sense to me. In the absence of starting from a text, we find clues in absolutely everything, from the space to the costumes, to actions people might come up with, even something they just saw in a shop or objects people left behind in the rehearsal studio. For *Club of No Regrets* (1993–4), it was the fact of having chalk scribbles all over the walls of the set – very brutal, very desperate – that helped us to find out about the people inside the piece, about who they were and about how they might move.

When did you start working in this way?
It's a process that has evolved. I'd say that over the years we've come to rely less and less on preconceived ideas and more and more on these complex accidents or discoveries made in the rehearsal studio. In the last few years the whole business of building spaces – of making them or rearranging them – has also become a part of what is presented on-stage, so the characters in *Emanuelle Enchanted* (1992) and those in *Hidden J* are all involved in building spaces, in manipulating the world they exist in.

What are your preoccupations as a director?
I am very interested in identity. I think about performance as a way of measuring yourself against other possibilities of yourself. Even in traditional theatre, actors want to measure themselves against the great roles. I think that people have always thought of performance as a way of playing with possible other versions of themselves, including things they fear. I'm fascinated with death too! I think death is the biggest ontological kernel of what theatre is about because it is the ultimate transformation. On stage deaths are not real: actors continue breathing. That's when you realize most fully that theatre really is composed of a physical body, a person in front of you, and a fiction, and the two are not the same. Theatre is a game that operates in between what is pretended and what is real.

Another of my concerns is to question what theatre is. Is it standing in front of a group of people who want you to do something? Why do people desire to see someone else perform? What is the performer's responsibility towards that? What is the fictional side of ourselves? I find that I try to explore these issues all the time.

Do you write your own texts?
Yes, largely. I often write large chunks of stuff and the performers then select the material depending on what they want to do; they might just take a line from page one, two from page three and one from page ten. Sometimes, as in *Speak Bitterness*, which started as an installation piece, it might happen that I don't write enough and then we all write more. A

lot of my work is based around the way people respond to each other; it's very important to me that not everything is preordained and that the actors and the audience work their way through the events we stage. So we do a lot of improvisation during the rehearsals which we record on video. Then, back home, we transcribe them into a kind of map which we try to edit, rearrange and recreate in performance. At times our work could be described as the attempt to recreate the discovery of an action that we had during the rehearsal phase.

How do you see your role as a director?
Sometimes I'm responsive, sometimes I lead things. I am like an organizer, a filter; but not a neutral filter, because ultimately it's what I like that is prioritized.

Has your notion of directing changed over the years?
I think that I used to be a control freak. Over the years, I've come to value what the performers do individually, what characterizes each performer and makes them different from anyone else.

I try to work with those differences, and in any case my directing develops within the ensemble – negotiating problems, finding new ways of approaching the work together. The core of the company has been together nearly fifteen years which is quite unusual, quite special.

What is most important to you about the way you work?
The idea of process, to go into a room and 'see what happens'; the fact that when you enter the room you have no idea whatsoever about what will happen. Unfortunately, there is a lot of pressure from the funding bodies to be competitive and describe your work way ahead in order to get subsidies. Funding bodies are not interested in the idea of an exploratory process. Unless you can describe in advance on a sheet of A4 what you are going to do you will never get any funding.

How does awareness of audience affect your work?
It depends on the project. To some extent I just work on the assumption that if something is interesting or fascinating to me then it will be interesting to other people too. However, all through the process we do little showings of work in progress, or previews, and we do take on board the feedback we get from people there. When we were doing *Nights in this City* (1995), a performance that took its audience on a guided tour of Sheffield, we did make calculations about what kinds of things the audience might be prepared to do for that kind of event. We discussed for a

while the possibility of getting people off the bus and leading them down a long darkened tunnel in a very run-down part of town, or of leading them up a very steep hill on foot to look down on the city, but we decided that there might be problems with that. We had to take into account the physical abilities of the audience, and how scared they might be.

Who and what have acted as influences on your work?
We were very influenced by Impact Theatre Co-operative who were the first people we saw making this kind of work in Britain. I've also been influenced by practitioners such as Pina Bausch, and the American company the Wooster Group. But what has influenced me most does not actually come from the theatre; my references and inspirations are very broad: Mark Smith's work with the punk band The Fall, Nicholas Roeg's cinema, especially *Performance*, Tarkovsky, fine art, films and performance art.

How do you see yourself in terms of the European theatrical landscape?
The strong literary theatre tradition in Britain does make life difficult for anyone working in a different way. In mainland Europe things are more open, more interesting, and so there have been plenty of opportunities for us there. In Britain the literary history gets championed at the expense of all others, and so time and again it feels like we're working in a vacuum. People often remark that what we're doing is 'shockingly new', but in fact it has a lineage and a context that is just too rarely known. The history of experimental theatre here in many ways is one of good artists being forgotten or marginalized before they ever get the funding or critical support that they need. At the middle to large scale the British have become great importers of new theatre from abroad – the Robert Le Pages of this world – but the record on taking home-grown innovation and really supporting it is very poor.

Do you feel that your work is rooted in Britain?
Yes, I think that we've been exploring the British landscape – not in a realist way, like the playwrights of the seventies, but in a contemporary expressionist way. It's a question of finding an appropriate form for describing a Britain in which two thirds of the culture is American television and fast-food. Alternatively, it's a question of finding an appropriate theatrical form to describe nearly two decades in which the north of England has not wanted a Conservative government but has been forced to suffer one – two decades of cultural alienation, of ruination.

The aesthetic of our work – scrappy, fragmented, discordant – has been very much born from the feeling of making-do, of the strange collisions between cultures, north and south, England and America, that one gets in a place like Sheffield.

Do you feel that you can work as you like in this country?
No. The climate for innovation is not very sympathetic. The framework for providing theatre in England hasn't really changed since the 1950s – a very patriarchal model based on big buildings and plays. The funding system is at the mercy of a repressive government and is consequently fixated on audience figures and touring targets. For younger artists it is harder and harder to draw unemployment money as a way of subsisting while developing their work – government regulations have tightened everything up. I think there'll be lots more solo work in the UK over the next few years – it's all people will be able to afford to make!

What would you hope to see developing in terms of the director and the directorial role in the next few years?
I'd like more space and time to work in an exploratory way – to reverse the pressure towards instant product. And I'd like to see the British theatre in general become much less insular – to recognize and explore its links to fine art, to performance, to film and so on instead of harping on endlessly about writing as if there was nothing in the theatre but words and writers.

JOHN FOX

John Fox was born in Hull in 1938. After national service in the Royal West African Frontier Force, he studied Philosophy, Politics and Economics at Oxford University and Fine Art at Newcastle University. In 1968, whilst lecturing in painting and performance art at Bradford and Leeds Colleges of Art, he co-founded Welfare State International with Sue Gill and others. He is also a printmaker, performer, bit part musician, poet and video-maker. In 1996 he wrote the libretto of *From Scratch*, a 'hiphopera' and song cycle composed by Luk Mishalle. His most notable pieces of site-specific celebratory events include: *Tempest on Snake Island* (Toronto, 1981, with Boris Howarth), a procession of tableaux linking Prospero and Canadian politics; *Raising the Titanic* (London, 1983), an allegorical sinking of western Europe engineered in a derelict dock; *King Real and the Hoodlums* (Barrow-in-Furness, 1983), a community film about senility and submarines scripted by Adrian Mitchell; *False Creek, A Visual Symphony* (Vancouver EXPO, 1986), parades, tableaux and focused performance depicting Pinocchio in the grip of mendacious capitalism; *Shipyard Tales* (Barrow-in-Furness, 1983–90); *Glasgow All Lit Up* (Glasgow, 1990); *Lantern Arcade* (Glasgow, 1994), an installation sculpture and *Lantern House* (Ulverston, 1994–8). Recent research into rites of passage includes *The Dead Good Funerals Guide* (Ulverston, 1996) and *The Dead Good Namings Guide* (Ulverston, 1999), both written with Sue Gill – poetic manuals of instruction for alternative funeral and naming rites. In 1998 he was awarded the Northern Electric 10th Anniversary Special Award for Outstanding Achievement in the Arts.

What is your principal medium?
The choice is determined by the occasion and need. The poetry grows from the site; the medium, which could be theatre, video, installation sculpture, architecture or a mixture of all these, changes accordingly. We have designed a ceremonial space for new rites of passage, *Lantern House* (1994–8), so in this case the principal medium is architecture and the principal materials are oak trees and cement. The form of *Lantern House* is a physical, practical artwork which functions at a number of levels: it is a sculpture, a physical poem where performances take place and where training is possible. Most of our work is multi-faceted and this

particular project is part of a bigger dream which is located somewhere in between aesthetics and social advocacy.

How would you describe your work?
As cultural activism in celebratory and imagist mode. Our most recent big creation, *Lantern House*, is taking place in the centre of our home town Ulverston, the birthplace of Stan Laurel. We have converted a Victorian school and tarmac car park into a wild oasis with a river, hanging gardens, fountains, a shadow theatre, a helter-skelter tower and traditional 'cruck' barn, workshops, furniture and an electronic beacon with world-wide web connections. It is a communications centre, an artwork in itself, and a joyous place to recuperate and create new art-works: a haven for the imagination. In our hinterland, in the no man's land between Wordsworth and Windscale, where people are trained to manufacture nuclear submarines or drugs, some of our imagery is based on Cumbrian mythology and the landscape of the Lake District, More-cambe Bay and beyond. The project is a constructed environment built on an existing building with a mythology linking our Cumbrian head-quarters with an international network of artists.

What else characterizes your work?
We try to respond spontaneously to real need rather than making gra-tuitous spectacles. In the course of our construction projects we make occasional ceremonies. For example, in early 1995 we invented a ritual of pouring concrete to make the floor of the wooden barn and buried a capsule with poems and fragments of the forest floor. When the thresh-old of the same barn was constructed we laid a broken dagger in the doorway trench. This dagger was an award from a Polish Theatre Festi-val which we were given at Wroclaw in 1975; it was a brass dagger bent back on itself to signify an end to war. Our then general manager, who is half Polish, spoke a ritual blessing in Polish asking that the space would only ever be used for peaceful co-operation.

We also had a 'topping-out' ceremony, a small ritual to celebrate the placing of ridge beams. In this case, as we placed an oak branch on the roof, we read special poems and the Ulverston Silver Band played 'Hearts of Oak'. About two hundred local residents were present to witness and enjoy the occasion. The barn is used for shadow puppetry, the gardens for story-telling. We have also constructed a portable cere-monial space for rites of passage to include namings, weddings and funerals.

How would you describe theatre in a simple way?
A place of wonder where wild and magical dreams come alive, whether on a hill top or in a quarry, by a lake or indoors; where singers, dancers, acrobats and wild creatures take you on a journey that's both fun and scary; an unforgettable place where you leave behind school uniforms, bullies and homework – a bit like holding a magnifying glass over the world so that everything appears to be exaggerated for a timeless moment.

What are the guiding principles of your directing practice?
Again, it varies according to the occasion and the scale. If I am working with hundreds of people under the pressure of a short deadline I am more autocratic than at other times.

I prefer to work by encouraging and stimulating people's talents in the way that a band leader might offer tunes and harmonies for people to explore. If there is time, I like the ideas to develop slowly through consensus, but if necessary I write detailed scenarios, instructions and words. I enjoy working with people and being surprised by the things they discover. If I want total control, which is rare these days, I make my woodcuts or leather shadow puppets and conceive and perform the whole exhibition or show.

In *Glasgow All Lit Up* (1990), which involved a parade of eight thousand people with ten thousand lanterns, there was huge scope for individual creativity because literally thousands of people were inventing their own lanterns. The organization was cellular and the main things we provided were the inspiration, the workshop leaders, the management structure, the materials and £330,000 of funding.

Lanterns can be constructed by anybody and vary from the smallest hand-held pyramid to truck-sized floats, but a consistency of materials (in this case willow sticks, tissue paper and candles) creates a certain aesthetic unity, whatever the scale of imagery. Here the framework was quite loose, but all the participants of a city and regional community network worked for eighteen months towards one evening parade.

In *Shipyard Tales* in Barrow-in-Furness (1983–90), I was more of an impresario leading from the back. Here we encouraged hundreds of local people, many from the shipyard, to write, produce and perform fourteen separate productions varying from docu-dramas to sit-coms and pantomimes to percussive percussions and carnival fire shows.

The case of *Lord Dynamite* (1991) was quite different again. This was a mythologized version of the life of Alfred Noble which I co-directed with Tim Fleming. It was designed as a touring show and was a landscape opera for repeated performances to audiences of one to three thousand. Here I wrote the words and songs with the playwright Kevin Fegan and gave strong staging instructions, but selected a regular team of experienced practitioners, performers, pyrotechnicians and engineers who I knew would interpret the idea with style and invention. Parts of the show were also designed so that there could be some community involvement via percussion bands and dancers. In many ceremonies and rites of passage we hand over the responsibility totally to the participants. At first, usually, they believe they cannot create for themselves and maintain they have never written poetry before, but with guidance they always discover hidden inner resources.

Although my directing method was very different in all these cases, the overall principle was and is to generate the maximum celebration and creativity so that all the people involved realize their own potential. Of course, I'd like to see this principle applied to wide society outside our theatrical fraternity.

How would you describe the way you work?
I am a wayward dreamer who thinks in images and needs to make his dreams concrete. Sometimes I chew on an idea for years but I prefer to be as spontaneous as circumstances allow. I try increasingly to play in the moment, but when I am working with others I enjoy working collectively, particularly with free imaginative spirits. At best my role is probably to have visions and inspire others.

What do you mean by vision or dream?
Something imagined that cries out to be made visible and concrete. This could be a flash of inspiration or a long-lasting obsession, a precise image or a feeling. It may originate in the imagination, but it soon grows and changes organically on the ground. For example, by demolishing an air raid shelter and digging up the concrete at our headquarters we revealed an underground river which flows across our property. Our desire paths shifted; the energy and sight of the water flow caused us to rethink the nature of a ceremonial space and the location of a proposed thirty-foot high musical wooden tower.

It's a bit like making a tapestry: you draw the tapestry first, then you fill it in with embroidery. You can decide as you go along that you could make the sky pink or green, but you've got to know that there will be a sky there in the first place. My job is to stretch the canvas and then sketch something on it which can then be coloured in and extended.

Has your notion of directing changed over the years?
I have learnt to listen and to wait. Also, the hinterland of our work has changed. Once I was more interested in a relatively closed organization. In the early street shows we used heavy make-up and masks which could be alienating and intimidating, and when we worked as jet-set jesters on the international festival circuit there was, maybe, some merit in avant-garde oddness.

Now we are much more open, because we work in Ulverston. This is a small town of twelve thousand people where so much has changed because of the decline of the shipyard industry and the partial collapse of the local economy, which has especially affected local shopkeepers. In Ulverston, I am interested in seeing how the whole town could regenerate, that is if it will regenerate, and as a resident and artist I am as concerned about the economic development of the town as its culture. The context for the work changes the way we work; for example, it's all very well making coffins, but if the local undertakers are not interested, then just designing coffins would make us élitist. Once you decide to work with people other than theatre-goers or artists, you have to find a language or a way of reaching people which is much broader. So when I say that I now listen more, I am not just listening to artists, but to the wider context, the wider rumours. I believe I direct in a more open and relaxed way than a few years ago, and I am more interested in the poetry under my feet, away from the fashionable arty backwaters.

How does awareness of audience affect your work?
In the public work totally. In the private intermittently. The notion of audience is tricky for me because it can be very passive. As our work has moved away from theatre and art circuits, large-scale spectacles and such spectator sport in general, we have discovered through carnivals, street processions, lantern festivals, seasonal gatherings and rites of passage and so on that people often prefer to become a participating congregation rather than a consuming audience. I use the word congregation guardedly because we are stage managers rather than priests.

Audiences also change, having different needs according to size and experience. In Ulverston, after seventeen years, our lantern parades have grown from three hundred to ten thousand townspeople who are now much more critical of the quality of the lanterns than they were before. The young people we taught in 1983 are now teaching their own children how to make lanterns.

On occasion, I still explore wilder imaginative ideas and use these as a basis for more contained work such as theatre pieces, woodcuts, poem books, song cycles or a script for others to interpret. I am like an inter-locutor or ferryman who invites the audience on a journey. Sometimes in good improvised performances the revealing and communicating happen simultaneously and the audience follow their trickster into mys-terious territory.

Who and what have acted as influences on your work?
My wonder came first as a nine-year-old making puppet shows and copying the transformations of Aladdin and Jack and the Beanstalk from the New Theatre in Hull. For years I didn't realize there was any other kind of theatre.

At the age of sixteen, inspired by Kid Ory and George Lewis, the Orleans musicians, I bought a clarinet. I still play corny soprano sax and prefer African roots music. Anger came later, with political satire about bad teachers in school revues.

Another major influence was military service as an impressionable eighteen-year-old in Ghana where drums played every night, tribal rit-uals were regular events and I danced to early Hi Life bands. Here I experienced non-Western culture for the first time, learned to use explosives in site-specific pretend battles, discovered poverty, a life expectancy of forty-seven in the Third World and came to loathe Christianity.

At Oxford University I discovered that the English class system was alive and vicious. I hated economics and preferred spending all my time either at the Ruskin School of Drawing where Geoffry Rhoades (an English Chagall) taught me to look and draw when I wasn't staying up all night to paint sets for experimental theatrical revues and numerous plays on proscenium stages.

The performers who influenced me are: Tommy Cooper, Frank Randall and the Goon Show. The poets are: Adrienne Rich, Raymond Carver, Bertolt Brecht, Norman Nicholson, Adrian Mitchell, William Blake, Tom Waits and Kenneth Patchen. The thinkers are: John Ruskin, William Morris and Thoreau and the rather discredited anthropologist Colin Turnbull.

I was also influenced by hundreds of figurative visual artists, from Nolde to Catalan frescoes, Facteur Cheval's home-made grotto, Gaudi's cathedral, Picasso's late works, aboriginal rock paintings, George Herriman (Krazy Kat), Munakata the Japanese woodcut printer, Fellini's films, *West Side Story*, November Fifth bonfires, Padstow May Day, the Gilles de Banche in Brussels, Balinese ceremonies and shadow theatre, Peter Schumann's Bread and Puppet Theatre, Albert Hunt, John Arden and Margaretta d'Arcy, the People Show, Dogtroep, the Grand Magic Circus, Punch and Judy, Bob Frith and his Horse and Bamboo Theatre, English fairgrounds, early American 'happenings' and Derek Jarman.

All these are inspirational, but in general I am unteachable and always have to make my own mistakes. I read voraciously and cannibalize books for ideas. And I probably learnt most from Sue and our children, Daniel, thirty, and Hannah, twenty-eight, and cookery books. Theatre is just like cooking: good ingredients well prepared and offered as a gift to willing guests.

How do you see yourself in terms of the European theatrical/performance landscape?

I don't think there is much connection at all. The movement for celebratory art in the community is growing, but it still often ends up as gratuitous spectacle. Our work is now more of a continuous process combined with vernacular art and with cultural generation than with theatrical or performance areas. On occasion, we have had superficial similarities with say El Comediants, Dogtroep or even Archaos and other French and Spanish theatre companies. Yet these companies still generally produce theatrical commodities, whereas we are clown agents for chaos in a wider context. As artists we visualize ideas through elaborate linked imagery, making comic utopias seem feasible. Our concerns are more social, holistic, ecological and anthropological than many performance-oriented companies in Europe. We make celebratory events with a social agenda and place our art in the community. Rites of passage are a long way from the festival circuit.

I guess that we are following obliquely in the footsteps of European carnival, theatrical vagabonds and surreal and Dada artists, but equally in the steps of European social reformers such as Morris, Ruskin and even Wilberforce.

We are, or were, clearly in the line of original rough Shakespeare, mummers' plays as rituals, mystery plays, fairground, maybe some circus, buskers, street bands and oral poets. We are generally in the area of popular contact entertainment, in the craft of music hall, and early Joan Littlewood in England. I think that our work is original and innovative because we put art and social change together in new patterns. I believe Armand Gatti was trying to do the same in France.

JOHN FOX

How would you describe celebratory theatre?
It's an attitude of mind: pathological optimism and ironic idealism. It's about enjoying life. Some people worry that it is only feel-good euphoria, but it is to do with a consistent value system.

Celebratory theatre includes carnivals, pyrotechnics and large-scale dance events, like some raves, or vernacular art, like house-building and rites of passage (including funerals) – events which allow us to celebrate our existence and work within the fabric of people's lives. Thirty years ago I never imagined I would be writing a book on the art of funerals or naming babies, but now I see it as part of the same preoccupation.

Do you feel you can work as you want to work in this country?
That's a very difficult question. We have almost gained enough of a reputation to do as we wish, but it has taken years. Funding bodies have tolerated us and often generously supported us in emergencies, but occasionally they have panicked and tried to force us to subscribe to existing funding guidelines and outmoded categories. Even the fashionable clichés such as 'multi-media' or 'cross-art forms', or 'live art', or 'site-specific installations', or 'outreach community art' or 'time-based art' are attempts to make definitions that exclude. We are now ploughing our own furrow because it is clear that we do good work and are not going to disappear. We were awarded over a million pounds in 1996 in our arts lottery bid, so the establishment must value our imagination and be keen for our theatre to evolve into architecture.

I do not like confrontation and reactive work, preferring to create positive artworks that are life-enhancing. We have managed to do this in England for over thirty years with many ups and downs. This journey is recorded in detail in our book *Engineers of the Imagination* by Baz Kershaw and Tony Coult. However, the signs are that, as we approach the millennium, many people are desperate for new ideas and new communities. My guess is that energy and collective consciousness are shifting dramatically. Possibly just as England was the first into the industrial revolution, it will be the first out!

We are looking for a new value structure, a culture which may be less materially based, but where more people will actively participate and gain the power to celebrate moments that are wonderful and significant in our lives. This new culture may include the building of our own houses, naming our children, burying our dead, dancing in Dionysian street festivals, announcing partnerships, marking anniversaries, creating secular sacred spaces and producing whatever drama, stories, songs, rituals, ceremonies, pageants and jokes are relevant to new values and new iconography. It is hard to do this in our current culture which is fixated on its historical heritage and nineteenth-century notions of work and religion. In our so-called free-market economy of consumerism and global expansionism attitudes are so institutionalized that any real pioneering innovation can be seen as a threat.

Even in your questions there is a certain hidden agenda, trying to understand the nature of directing. I think that we live in a society where people are typecast and forced into narrow channels and specialisms where they can't communicate with each other. I think that this presumption is divisive rather than encompassing. Your questions come from a certain presumption and answering them allows the presumption to continue. So, in a sense, a book like this could be part of the problem.

What are your obsessions as a director?
I like to make dreams come alive. I like to think that I can create an alternative way of living, a strong joyful island which is a little separate from the mainstream.

As a director my obsession is achieving the impossible in my own lifetime and ensuring that we document everything. I am also obsessed with trying to run the company democratically without hypocrisy; trying to balance my ego and still give freedom to others. Otherwise I don't like to distinguish between the director and me, John Fox. As a person I am obsessive by nature and therefore overwork. I don't think that I have lofty and worthy obsessions, just scores of banalities such as Mr Punch, skeletons, lighthouses, eggs, herons, lanterns, towers, wheels of fire, woodcocks, ziggurats, ladders, blocks of flats, ice giants, bicycle theatre and worlds within worlds (especially the convention of crescent moons in comic-strip balloons). I'm also obsessed with the sea, shacks on the beach and shacks in the head; death; cyclical rebirth; books; boxes full of unfiled souvenirs; taking notes on paper; getting rid of priests; and, above all, believing that art can give people truth, energy and confidence to change deadness.

What would you hope to see developing in terms of the director and their role in the next few years?
I don't want to separate directors from everything else. I don't like high priests. I'd like to see a society which values creativity a lot more and where more people have a valued place in it. If more people want to do

theatre, more people should have a chance to be directors. Too many people want to become 'famous directors'. I would actually like to see directors respect their colleagues more and facilitate group creation. I see this as an educational process with political implications where we all draw out each others' dreams and poetry and where we could all laugh a lot more in an equal and open society.

DAVID GLASS

David Glass was born in Switzerland in 1957. He has performed solo work for over eighteen years in over forty countries and has directed work for dance, theatre and opera companies around the world. He founded the David Glass Ensemble in 1988. The Ensemble has performed *Popeye in Exile* (1990–93), *Bozo's Dead* (1991), the first theatre adaptations of *Gormenghast* (1992 and still on international tour), *Les Enfants du Paradis* (1993, Cambridge Theatre Company), *The Mosquito Coast* (1994–5, Nuffield Theatre, Southampton) and a music theatre production of *La Dolce Vita* (1996, Crucible Theatre, Sheffield). In 1995 and 1996 Glass toured his show *Lucky*. In 1993 he won the Martini/TMA Regional Theatre Award for Best Director with *Gormenghast*. He was movement director for the Clive Barker film *Nightbreed* (1986), and assistant director on the feature film *Beg!* (1994) shown at the Sundance Film Festival in America. Currently, he is working on The Lost Child Trilogy: *The Hansel Gretel Machine* (1998), *The Lost Child* (1999) and *The Red Thread* (1999/2000).

What is your starting-point as a director?
I start with the heart of the story I am trying to tell, or the theme I am exploring. The stories have varied sources: for instance, *Gormenghast* (1992–5) came from Mervyn Peake's book and *Enfants du Paradis* (1993) was inspired by Marcel Carné's film. I let the style of the performance be defined by the content of the story and allow the theatrical language to grow during the creative process. *Gormenghast*, which I see as a Gothic melodrama, is a hybrid book and I wanted the hybridity of styles reflected in the show; Peake grew up in China and I turned to kabuki for its simplicity and sparseness of style for ideas on how I might direct it. I was searching for a transformation of the figures in a highly formalized space, and Far Eastern methods and techniques of approaching performance seemed an appropriate way to explore the story. Throughout my work on a show I am always seeking a language which expresses the content of the story. A writer is concerned with both the internal and external expression of a story, and as a director I strive to reconcile the complexity of form and content.

My performance *Lucky* (1995) was more thematically based; it was an exploration of what it is like to be inside the head of an autistic boy. I knew that because this was an internal exploration the theatrical language could not be verbal, so I developed a theatre language based on atmosphere and emotions expressed through the body. I had worked with autistic children some years previously and found myself both fascinated and troubled by them.

Do you spend long periods on research?
Yes, the research can take years, and it's for this reason that the company tends to do one major show and one small-scale show a year, always on things that I will have been thinking about for some time. I must have watched Fellini's film *La Dolce Vita* at least sixty times and read all the material I could before I embarked on my stage exploration of it. *Les Enfants du Paradis* and *Popeye* (1990–93) each involved two years of research. For *Lucky* the director Rae Smith and I visited centres and read a great deal of material on autism. The performances are meticulously hand-crafted and I usually have an eight-week rehearsal period.

How important is the design concept in your work?
I forge close relationships with designers, and often work with artists like Ralph Steadman. I form very specific design concepts before I start work on rehearsals. In *La Dolce Vita* (1996), for example, I was exploring concepts of masculine and feminine through line and shape, and seeking ways of mapping the complex sexual politics of 1950s Italy on to the design. Fellini's *La Dolce Vita* was influenced by Dante's *Divine Comedy* and I used symbolic colour coding to convey fundamental ideas: red, for instance, represented earthly love, and blue represented spiritual love. With *Gormenghast* I wanted to find ways of conveying the claustrophobia of that world, and I experimented with spatiality and how it could be worked to create atmosphere. The seven doors I used created a sense of imbalance and were too many for the audience to absorb at once. I wanted to create a world on stage that could also exist in the imaginations of the audience. I believe that literalization is anathema to theatre, and that it is vital to let an audience have imaginative room of their own. I read *Gormenghast* as a teenager and see it as a book about a rite of passage: characters are caught in the same world but they do not help one another, instead they battle against each other and suffer. I wanted to capture the ritual of story-telling, so I made the staging, the acting and the colours highly stylized. Until the flood at the end of the play the

dominant colour was black; but the Chinese white cloth, the flood, was representative of change and purity: the play moves from black, no change, to white, absolute change. These visual metaphors are an inherent part of the form and the story-telling, and I spend a lot of time with a designer discussing how to capture them. These discussions often take place before the show is written: text is one part of the theatre world and writing can form one important element of structure, but to assume that text is the main body of theatre is to limit the possibilities of creating a rich visual world.

How do you work in the rehearsal room?
At the beginning of the rehearsal process I draw a model for the actors and explain that the body of each actor is like an etching plate; the process of rehearsal etches choices and possibilities into their bodies. At the end of the rehearsal they have many ways of exploring the piece on stage. That night's performance is the result of many weeks of work; it is structurally similar to the previous night's performance, but the feel is totally different. Like a run of prints, each of the performances looks similar to the another but is in fact very different. Actors have to develop a sense of group corporeality and group imagination, and I retrain Western actors to develop the animality and energy that goes with ensemble work. It's not a training they are accustomed to, and individual performers realize how alienated they normally are from other performers on stage. By the end of the eight weeks they should be able to move together like gazelles, though often this sensitivity doesn't emerge until the performance proper.

At the start of the rehearsal day a one and a half hour class is taken by the performers. This is done first to clear away the detritus that accrues in performers, and second to stimulate levels of physical, emotional and imaginative stamina, which I find to be very low in British performers. These classes involve very direct and physical contact and bring about a tremendous closeness in the company; they also enable me to understand each individual body and the way they work. I often finish with a Noh clapping meditation.

Every show requires its specific map for rehearsals. For *La Dolce Vita* I followed the initial work-out with a music class. In the afternoons I generally lead ensemble games such as group competitions or chorus work. I'm very methodical and layer the classes, dividing the day into four or five one and a half hour periods. I find that this is a good length for concentration. Performers like structure, and discipline is a means of giving security in a positive, supportive way. The demands of each group of performers are different and there is no fixed way to proceed, but by investing time in training you feed the actors on every level: spiritual, physical and emotional. Without this the actors use resources and ideas that they've tried and tested, and work can become superficial and directionless. For *Gormenghast* I ran a class on the exploration of Gothic melodrama. I played imaginative games that linked in with the themes, rhythms and world of the piece; and I spent the last part of the day concentrating on text, taking it scene by scene, examining meaning and dividing it into units of action. I often work by giving my actors a series of imaginative choices; for example, I ask them to repeat a scene imagining that it is raining, or cold, or unbearably hot. In this way the colour of a play can move a lot but it provides a richness of texture and vocabulary that is critical. Initially, I work on movement, text and music separately, creating a palette for the actors to draw from – the director must allow for actors to have the freedom to explore these areas for themselves.

What does the word 'director' mean to you?
On the simplest level the director is the organizer of space, time and bodies. The complex level of directing is dealing with sensitive individuals and their psychic lives. Certain subject matters can be delicate and the psyche is vulnerable; delving below the surface of the conscious mind can release enormous creative energy but it can also release psychoses and problems. As a director you must be alert to all this and know how to manage it. In my twenties I didn't direct because I simply didn't have enough experience of life myself to know how to handle the other actors' psyches.

I have an imagination that I can lose myself in, but I have to fuse my imagination together with that of the ensemble, whilst remembering that ultimately the imaginations of the audience will enter into the performance as well. My job as director is quite distinct: it brings with it an energy of its own and has a strong organic effect on the performers. What is important is that we – the performers, designers, writers, composers etc. – have a shared vision. It is this vision that a director must constantly focus on.

Could you elaborate on the importance of the imagination in your work?
I think we underestimate why imagination exists at all, and in teaching I think imagination is undervalued and underused. We tend not to ques-

tion the effect of the outer world on the inner world and vice versa. Emotions are felt in the body and this connects with our needs and desires. If I cannot *imagine* wanting a cup of coffee then I will not be able to act it effectively. Emotion and imagination are what connect the inner and outer worlds and this makes the imagination a powerful tool for transforming both ourselves and the world around us. The imagination is fluid and reflects the inner fluidity of our lives: one moment we can be sad, the next happy. Theatre is the celebration of every moment as it is happening, and it is the job of the director to get every actor to play each moment fully whilst ensuring that once played each moment is also let go.

This facility to let go is very hard to acquire, but the control of the ego is vital in ensemble work. I bring Buddhist methods into my training to try to cultivate a certain detachment in actors, a detachment that Lecoq might refer to as the neutral mask. I'm interested in getting actors to work together, but if an actor doesn't *want* to do this their ego will prevent them being able to give to the group. For this reason, time for play has to be worked into the rehearsal process. Play is a necessary process that humans go through in order to be able to deal with an incomprehensible and contradictory world: children come to terms with danger through play; they confront death, isolation, war. Play is risk and pain. At the same time play is pleasurable, it is fun, it enables socialization and a move into adulthood. In the body of the child joy and pain are intertwined, and it is this state that the actor has to be able to reach. As the director I have to try to unlock the performers, and this involves unlocking pain, but the ego tries to stop itself from suffering. Buddhist teaching describes nature as inherently playful and argues that suffering is inevitable and must happen: all the individual can do is let go of the need to suffer; refuse the desire and one suffers less. I see a parallel with this in terms of play and imagination in rehearsal. We need ego to control ourselves and the world around us, but we need an ego that is strong, colourful, compassionate and open. If I find actors like this then the work is wonderful, but it is rare to find such people.

What I am describing here is a philosophy of teaching actors and of directing, which is coloured by my own training and background. I would argue that there are few inspiring teachers/directors because most are interested in an industry, in mainstream commercial theatre, and I have not gone down that route. In my opinion theatre which is solely concerned with industry strokes the ego rather than making it question itself; it means that actors are not challenged beyond certain narrow constraints, are not encouraged to explore their imaginative and creative potential.

What bearing does music have in your work?
It's very important to me. Eisenstein created a line of imitation in art: at one end was pure abstraction; and at the other was literalization. My style of theatre-making employs a symbolism which moves towards abstraction. Music, however, is the one art form that is not imitative of anything else; it does not represent anything and is therefore a wholly abstract form. When the body moves to music it begins to imitate something that is man-made. A child imitating music becomes like the music. This realm of the non-literal, of dance, is wonderfully liberating; the observer does not know what the dancer is doing, but even so can feel connected to something spiritual, to something abstract.

Music evokes very powerful emotions, and a song can be the closest we come to describing how the world feels. Verbalization has its roots in emotion: we might describe the vowel sounds as the emotion of words, and the consonants as the elements that define those emotions. I see song as an extension of this vowel/consonant relationship.

I often tell my actors that there are two things to play with in performance: shape, which exists in space; and rhythm, which exists in time. Through the use of shape and rhythm we measure out time. Rhythm relates to our emotional state: the beat of the heart and the rhythm of the breath. I use meditation exercises to try to instil a sense of inner rhythm in actors.

Who and what have acted as influences on you?
I saw a great deal of circus and carnival acts as a boy. I observed Peter Brook's work when I was in Paris and it influenced me strongly. Marcel Marceau, Jean-Louis Barrault, my training at the Lecoq Mime School and Ariane Mnouchkine all had an impact on me. The strongest theoretical influences on my work have been Stanislavski, Brecht and Artaud: Stanislavski gives us a language for the exploration of storytelling and character; Brecht gives us insights into the relation between the performance and the audience and posits a simple but very effective style of theatre; Artaud points us back to emotion and psyche as the roots of performance. Practitioners such as Grotowski have also been very important, and so has my study of theatre forms like Kathakali and

Japanese Noh. I have benefited from a mentor and friend in Mike Alfreds and find it positive to have older, experienced practitioners with whom I can talk about my work.

Are you aware of changes in your approach to directing over the years?
I've come to understand that a good director is someone who has the ability to take a frame and place it over a detail or a fragment of the whole picture. The more specific I am in what I examine, the more precise I can be in my work with actors. So I have changed in the sense that I have developed the stamina and the patience to plunge further into the work whilst striving for simplicity. If I ask my actors to be without ego I must demand it of myself. I too have to let go of my need to dominate events, it can be all too easy for a director to become a martinet. Life in theatre is a *life* for me and not a career; it is a means by which I explore myself.

Are you satisfied with the creative evolution of your company?
I have felt that my work is increasingly misunderstood by critics in this country. The audience loved *La Dolce Vita*, but the message from the critics is that England is not the place for this kind of work. I find that fundamental intellectual aspects of my work are not perceived by critics at all, as though they are baffled by theatre-making which does not conform to certain traditions. The company is artist led: each collaborator from writer to performer is encouraged to strive and to question, and because of this 'satisfaction' is rarely something the company or I feel. I think frustration is closer to the mark.

The company is at present going through a period of change and re-evaluation. It has been established for ten years, and there have been some successes and some failures. But now I'm taking eighteen months out to prepare for the next project and to reassess where we have got to. The next project will deal with the theme of lost children. It looks at how children deal with the loss of other children through death, famine, prostitution and war. We live in times of crisis and tragedy where children are concerned: we as adults fail them constantly and sink into deeper and deeper despair at the thought. We also increasingly have a sense of our own lost childhood with the stress and pressures of modern life. I intend to travel to three different areas of the world: South America, Africa and Asia. There I hope to work with local children and listen to their stories and discover their imaginative ways of dealing with the losses in their lives. I see the end performance as an imaginative fairy-tale, using the children's words and their work as the centre of our story-telling. The intention is that the company will act as the interpretative tool of children who have no voice. I am well aware of the political sensitivity of the project and of the need to protect these children and ourselves as a company. The project hits a chord in everyone I've spoken to, and I often notice a gesture of shame in myself or in the person I am talking to when I speak of it, as though we are guilty about what we have done to these children and to the child in ourselves.

What are your thoughts on audience?
The relationship between the performer/s and the audience interests me most about theatre, and it is only through this relationship that a piece of work begins to have some sort of sense. I spent two to three years doing street theatre after I finished studying in Paris, and became intrigued by the dynamic between the watcher and the watched: the watched subject has a need to be watched; in turn the watcher has a need to observe but to appear detached from what they are observing. Both performer and audience gain pleasure from this activity. I think this reflects a state of early childhood in which adults watch the child, who absorbs everything about the world around them including the gaze of the adults. Likewise, the gaze of the audience fills every moment with meaning for a performer, gives them élan, makes them feel enlivened; meanwhile an individual in the audience can feel loved by a performer even though the performer is not looking at them at all. Relationships between the observed subject and the observer are reflexive in a highly complex and interesting way.

I draw a parallel between infant and mother. The first thing we do in life is mirror our mother. Aristotle spoke of poetry, music and dance as the imitation of life, and it is through imitation, through a spirit of play that an infant learns about the world. Imitation is our first act of relating to others; it is an affirmation of being alive. Children wither spiritually if they are not loved, and similarly adults shut down emotionally if they do not have loving relationships. A relationship between performer and audience affirms a basic life instinct. I often make my actors play a game with a stick. I ask them both to give and receive the stick: these acts are very personal and the stick becomes the excuse to affirm relationships between performers. If a director does not understand the complexity of all these relationships in a performance they will not understand the spark of the play, of theatre itself.

Teaching is very important to you. Why?

What is removed in teaching is the need to have an end product: the concern is with pure process. As a teacher you lead the pupil through something which you yourself are exploring. The learning process is two-way, and I learn as much from my students as they learn from me.

I've taught in many different countries and what I find constantly fascinating is the way in which emotional archetypes are expressed through the body in similar ways the world over. With 'joy', for example, the mouth opens, the arms are thrown up and there is a clockwise rotation in the body. I could describe movements for grief, sadness, anger and so on. A short while ago I led a workshop on the rediscovery of the child, and the actors experienced a real catharsis: of wonder, of crisis, of creativity. They felt a tremendous sense of discovery.

Can you work as you want to in England?
I see work with the company as a series of explorations, and the grace that the actors have shown in trying to find new ways of working has been very rewarding. The company is held in high esteem, but I do grow weary of lip-service and lack of funds. I know, however, that my work makes a difference to the theatrical life of the country, and performers that have trained and worked with us are very much sought after. I see my work in the tradition of Lindsey Kemp, Shared Experience, Theatre de Complicite and DV8. We're all trying to discover different theatre languages, and we all connect strongly with the zeitgeist of the 1990s. I look back on the eighties as a tremendously destructive period for the arts, and I despair of the losses we made. There seems to be very little experimental theatre work happening now, and ticket sales have come to dictate artistic decisions too much of the time.

I hope that my theatre company will still exist in ten years' time but I do have doubts about survival. I sometimes feel that there will be a virtual apocalypse of English theatre, and that we will end up only with five to ten major theatre companies in the country.

How would you like to develop as a director?
I would hate to limit myself to anything. I love working with different media and there's nothing that I wouldn't consider. I have lives as a performer, a writer and a director, and generally I keep them separate from one another, though sometimes they do meet up. I've always looked outwards, beyond England. The company has always toured, and I think this is vital as certain elements in society become increasingly xenophobic. I hold on to the company with infinite care; it is precious; it

is fragile; much that I do is misunderstood – but it has a value, and I am committed to upholding that value, especially in a climate that has lost touch with a basic humanity. I am committed not only to the artistic ethos of the Ensemble, but also to the idea of a company who live and work together, who shout, laugh and cry together; by the end of a tour a greater humanity has been engendered in all of us. I place my hope in young talent and in all the fresh energy I see. As a director I must make myself as vulnerable and as open as I expect my performers to be. In this way I remain fresh and alive to the changing demands of the work.

LIVERPOOL JOHN MOORES UNIVERSITY
LEARNING SERVICES

GARRY HYNES

Garry Hynes was born in Ballaghaderreen, County Roscommon, Ireland. She founded Druid Theatre Company in 1975 with Mick Lally and Marie Mullen and was Artistic Director from 1975 to 1990. Her productions included *The Playboy of the Western World* (1975, 1982), M. J. Molloy's *Wood of the Whispering* (1983), Tom Murphy's *Bailegangaire* (1985) and *Conversations on a Homecoming* (1985), and John Ford's *'Tis a Pity She's a Whore* (1985). In 1986 she began to direct for the Abbey Theatre, where her productions included *A Whistle in the Dark* (1986) by Tom Murphy and *King of the Castle* (1989) by Eugene McCabe. In 1988 she directed *Man of Mode* by George Etheridge and *The Love of the Nightingale* by Timberlake Wertenbaker for the Royal Shakespeare Company at Stratford and London. Hynes was Artistic Director of the Abbey Theatre from 1991 to 1994 and her productions during that time included Sean O'Casey's *The Plough and the Stars* (1991), John McGahern's *The Power of Darkness* (1991) and *Famine* (1994) by Tom Murphy. In 1996 she directed *The Beauty Queen of Leenane* by Martin McDonagh in a Druid Theatre Company/Royal Court co-production, *The Loves of Cass Maguire* by Brian Friel for Druid and *Portia Coughlan* by Marina Carr for The Abbey. In 1997 she directed *The Leenane Trilogy* in a Druid/Royal Court co-production, while *The Beauty Queen of Leenane* transferred to Broadway, where it earned her a Tony Award for directing, the first woman to be so honoured.

What is your principal medium in theatre?
My starting-point is text. As a teenager I felt alienated from Irish literature of any kind, whether poetry, prose or drama. In the late sixties and early seventies I felt no connection with a specifically Irish tradition of writing and theatre, even though by that time I had become involved in theatre as a student at University College, Galway. I became involved in the drama society without knowing what I was doing. There was certainly no formal training: drama was the poor relation of the Faculty of English. During that time I travelled widely and worked consecutive summers in New York where I saw the work of people on the New York scene, including Joe Chaikin, Paul Foster and Meredith Monk. When a group of us set up Druid Theatre in 1975 my desire was simply to con-

tinue doing plays, and any notion of becoming a professional theatre company seemed remote and exotic. We found that our theatre was a strong telling of the West of Ireland and quite different to theatres in Dublin or London because our lives were different. When we started out we rejected plays that had already been staged in Dublin, because we wanted to proffer a different repertoire.

It was only when I directed J. M. Synge's *The Playboy of the Western World* (1975), which was an extraordinary experience for all of us involved, that I lost my scepticism and realized that such texts could have profound resonances with me. On the opening night I made a commitment to do the play again, which I did in 1982. My 'discovery' of Synge led me to look at the Irish repertoire and to playwrights such as M. J. Molloy, whose work blossomed in the forties and fifties. Tom Murphy, who is originally from County Galway, became an associate writer of Druid Theatre in 1985 and we have worked together very fruitfully.

How do you see your role as director?
I love the research aspect of a play. I think and I imagine, I look at paintings, listen to music, watch people; it's a process of absorbing stimuli and detail and might be a short or a long time. I have long relationships with actors – Druid worked as an ensemble of six to seven actors from 1979 to 1988, and I may start talking about a piece of work years before I make the decision to direct it. Gradually, I clarify my ideas on casting. My collaboration with the designer is vital and is absolutely a collaboration in that two imaginations explore both the visual and dramatic landscape of a play; I have a set of ideas in my mind which are never realized in the model, but seeing the model sparks off other ideas immediately and I begin to see people moving in the space. I can only describe this as a feeling I have of following something, as an instinct that I have. The same thing happens in the rehearsal room. I watch the actors like a hawk to try to read what is happening. Sometimes I feel like an editor: something happens to which I respond and in articulating that response the process can go deeper. In a sense a very real part of the process is the series of conversations which happen right up until the first night. In the rehearsal room I am an *agent provocateur* as well as the person who seeks to create problem-solving situations for actors. For me the work with actors is very much about stripping down the layers of meaning in a text so that the actor can arrive at a point where they have the clearest possible understanding of the play and their part in it.

A performance is at its best when things are at their purest. I am struck more and more by the fact that what I am directing and what the actor is acting is not the thing in itself but a judgement. A character will cry because their purse is stolen and I'll think she's over-reacting. As a director I have to be acutely aware of my opinions and try to make sure that they do not intrude; sometimes the line is so thin I don't know that I'm making a judgement. This is where the best actors are able to point out what I am doing. The absolute purity or simplicity of great acting is always shocking. When an actor says, 'I don't know' in response to a question or when an actor speaks the line, 'I love you' I realize that there are towering structures and assumptions built up round every word and thought. Only the most extraordinary craftsmen can work at the edge of our presumption. In Tom Murphy's play *A Whistle in the Dark* an old man stands on a chair in the last scene; it's a simple action but when you arrive at that point it's a monumental moment.

Why is theatre important to you?
The fact that a group of people are willing to meet at the same time in the same place on the understanding that they all want to share in an imaginary process is always an extraordinary thing to me. At its worst it is empty routine, but at its best theatre is a transcendent experience.

What has your experience of audience been with Druid Theatre Company?
In the early eighties we began to tour. Before then we'd been playing in formal venues such as arts centres, and we found that there were certain kinds of audiences we just weren't reaching. We started to take our work to places which had no professional venues and we found completely new and remarkable audiences. Those who are accustomed to theatre behave in certain ways and have a certain set of expectations; questions of class, dress code, behaviour and attitude become predictable. But if you change the nature of your audience you change the nature of the work you do and keep a sense of freshness and excitement. On tour in more remote areas we found that we often sold blocks of eight or nine tickets and played to extended families. These audiences are vastly different from those in large towns and cities.

Druid mostly performs in English, but we've found that on the islands the bi-lingual members of the company have spontaneously slipped in and out of English and Irish. This was *ad hoc*, and a result of actors and audience making a deep connection. In my opinion you can only justify yourself as a director, and justify any theatrical act, if the vitality of the play is of the present moment. If the work is not of the moment it is nothing, and the constant exposure of work to different audiences is part of the process of nurturing that vitality. At Druid we also ensured that we toured abroad and built up new audiences outside Ireland in cities like Glasgow, Sydney and London.

Has your notion of directing changed over the years?
I have a growing sense of the primacy of the actor. I talked earlier about 'stripping down' text, but this also applies to all the elements of a performance for me. Less is more, and something that might have excited me ten years ago can now seem intrusive or baroque. The space you create for the play is fundamental; if you don't create the right space nothing will be right. By space I mean the playing area, the architecture of the theatre, and the place that building occupies in the community, whether it's a front room or a West End pavilion. I directed Martin McDonagh's *The Beauty Queen of Leenane* (1996) in the Town Hall Theatre of Galway. The Irish recognized a drawing on tradition from plays of the thirties, forties and fifties, but they also soon realized that all was not as it seemed, and the black humour of the piece flowed. When the same play transferred to the Royal Court Theatre Upstairs in London the initial response was fundamentally different. The audience did not recognize the comedy or the tradition and placed the play in the tradition of Ibsen and Strindberg. This had a great deal to do with the position of the Royal Court in the theatre landscape of London. Different audience experiences of a play are like a great river; it may look the same, but there are different currents and depths in the water and the geography changes according to the interaction of actors and audience.

I am also more conscious of the form of theatre. Actors and audience are both engaged in a very powerful act of imagination; we all *pretend* that something is happening, and if this formal aspect of the process is not apparent theatre becomes deadly.

Where would you situate Druid Theatre Company?
The value of a theatre company must be global. If Druid isn't a European company determined by the specifics of its own existence then it has no right to exist at all.

Who has influenced your work?
It's difficult to say. I'd been in the business for five or six years when journalists began to ask me specifically about being a woman director, and I realized that it was unusual in Ireland. My imagination is fed by a

myriad of sources. I'm especially conscious of Peter Brook's work and his book *The Empty Space*. I saw a lot of theatre in New York during the seventies, which brought down a particular set of attitudes I had formed about theatre: I remember watching an action in the Performing Garage which the audience had to follow round. I'm also a great admirer of the sheer theatricality of Ariane Mnouchkine's work. One of the most thrilling moments of my life was listening to a song in a Mnouchkine play; it was a moment when I felt part of a rhythm greater than myself, a moment specific to me but in which I did not feel solitary. In the best theatre experiences the individual spectator is not solitary.

Do you feel you can work as you want to?
In terms of economic constraints I have been in a fortunate position. I have run theatres and chosen what I wanted to do. It's also a responsibility, and now that I'm half way through a career in the theatre I am very conscious that the world does not need yet another production of a classic play without a very good reason indeed. These days I see little point in doing a great many established plays. Why do the 900th production of *The Cherry Orchard*? What could I possibly offer? I am committed to new writing and currently find it vital and exciting.

What are your hopes for future theatre in Ireland?
Currently Ireland has an extraordinary reputation for new writing, but my feeling is that the concerns are small; I would like to see the canvas become broader and the influences more varied. I am certainly committed to new writing, and unless others show a willingness to work on new plays then theatre will disappear. At the moment I feel writers and actors in Ireland are all straddling a middle range. It would be marvellous if a new writer or actor emerged of such distinction that widespread attention was captured.

PHYLLIDA LLOYD

Born in Bristol in 1957, Phyllida Lloyd read Drama and English at the
University of Birmingham from 1976 to 1979. Her most notable pro-
ductions include: Emile Zola's *Earth* (Edinburgh Festival, 1985); *The
Comedy of Errors*, García Lorca's *Dona Rosita the Spinster* and Ten-
nessee Williams's *A Streetcar Named Desire* (Bristol Old Vic, 1989);
Wole Soyinka's *Death and the King's Horseman*, Euripides' *Medea*, *The
Winter's Tale* and Richard Sheridan's *The School for Scandal* (Manches-
ter Royal Exchange, 1990–91); Thomas Shadwell's *The Virtuoso* and
Aleksandr Ostrovsky's *Artists and Admirers* (Royal Shakespeare Com-
pany, 1991–2); John Guare's *Six Degrees of Separation* (Royal Court,
1992); Terry Johnson's *Hysteria* (Royal Court, 1993 and 1995); *Pericles*,
Joe Orton's *What the Butler Saw*, William Congreve's *The Way of the
World* (Royal National Theatre, 1994–5); Bertold Brecht's *The Three-
penny Opera* (Donmar Warehouse, 1991); Alexis-Emmanuel
Chabrier's *Opera L'étoile* (Opera North, 1991); Puccini's *La Bohème*
(Opera North, 1996); Benjamin Britten's *Gloriana* (Opera North, 1994
and Royal Opera House, 1997) and Luigi Cherubini's *Medée* (Opera
North, 1996).

How would you define theatre?
Theatre is a live performance by one group of people for another. The
audience enter into a pact with the actors to believe what is happening.
It's a matter of faith. Someone dies on stage, or three actors play a cow
in labour and give birth to a calf – the audience know it's not really happening, but through their faith in the event and the actors' belief in
their powers of transformation, something akin to magic may occur.
Each group knows that the other is there because of it and each audience member knows that they are not alone.

What is a director?
The director is the link between one world and the other; like a
medium, the director is there to unblock all the channels and to imagine
how one world (the audience) might be perceiving the other (the production). As if she were the captain of a spaceship landing on the earth
from another planet, the director wonders: Who are they? Who are we?
What have we got to tell them and how best can we express ourselves?

In rehearsal the director watches the story unfold, listening from the edge of the circle. The director has gone ahead, explored the territory, chosen the best people for the expedition, but can never predict just how the journey will unfold.

What is your major preoccupation as a director?
In 1989 I was awarded a scholarship to go to the former Soviet Union to watch Russian and Georgian theatre directors in rehearsal. It was a crucial time historically, because although the system was beginning to unravel, the legacy of extraordinary continuity was visible everywhere. On the one hand I had a sense of theatre having been Church and Parliament; of great theatre actors with more status than the Mayor of Leningrad. On the other hand, the system protected dull people perpetuating dull ideas in jobs from which they could not be sacked. There were interminable rehearsal periods in which nobody could remember why they had begun working. At best there was a belief that to be an actor or a director required a lot of learning; that a production was a difficult thing to achieve. Great directors, many of whom taught in theatre schools in tandem with producing plays, had formed companies out of classes of graduating students and had stayed together for periods as long as fifteen years. The level of trust in each other, faith in the process of rehearsal and richness of their performance was astounding.

That same year I directed a new play by an American writer. It had been a big hit in New York and expectations were high. The writer arrived in London for our first run through, and after watching the performance announced that two of the actors 'would have to go': if they weren't 'cooked' by now (after three weeks of rehearsal) they would never be. Of course this was a Broadway 'fire first, ask questions later' approach, focused only on the result and with no understanding that we were mid-way between two points, that things would grow and change daily, not just until the dreaded press night, but beyond.

After these experiences I began to see much of what I do as poised between two places – between packaging and process. In England, we still have weekly repertory in our collective memories, and directors and actors have evolved into resourceful creatures who can make things happen quickly and with great skill: we're ripe for seduction by the 'wham-bam, wrap it up and sell it school'. We also share some of the faith in the long quest with our neighbours in the East. It is this tension between allowing something to happen in the rehearsal room and, on the other hand, grabbing it, shaping it and fixing it – that's my preoccupation.

Has your notion of directing changed over the years?
One of the Georgian directors I met asked me how many plays I had directed. When I answered 'twenty-two', he replied: 'That should never have been allowed to happen.' In his view, I should have done the same play twenty-two times or four plays five times each. In 1989 I thought this was curious – now I understand what he meant. I only ever feel as if I'm doing the job properly when doing something for a second time.

What is your principal medium?
I've always worked with text and music. I've worked on new plays, operas and 'classical' plays, by which I mean those that have become established in the repertoire, often containing heightened language. Recently I have begun to work with actors and contemporary dancers to see what happens when sophisticated signs and complex language come together.

What interests you most in the notion of process?
Process is full of tangible and intangible phases, and each of them excites me differently. The time spent before rehearsals begin, exploring the architecture of the play, often with the designer, is like amassing supplies for the journey – planning the route if you like. Being part of a new group of people and forging out into unknown territory with them in rehearsal is a fantastic privilege; so is entering cultural and social worlds, touching upon emotional experiences that one might otherwise only glimpse at through years of travel or psychoanalysis. Even the technical phase of a production, which can render everything that has seemed natural and clear, cluttered and mechanical, can be a thrilling phase if the collision of actors, space, light and sound is correct.

What role does collaboration play in your work?
I'm of a generation of directors that tend to work in a more collaborative way. This has nothing to do with gender; it just reflects the history of the master–slave relationship in the twentieth century. The business world realizes it can get more out of its workers by collaborating with them, rather than beating the hell out of them. I know that many great productions are born out of frightful conflict, but I just don't enjoy working from a position of siege. It doesn't help me to think clearly. I like to make the rehearsal room a safe place in which dangerous things can occur.

What are the guiding principles of your directing practice?
Theatre can be all manner of things: a plea for tolerance, a rallying cry

or an evening of downright silliness, but whatever it is, it should effect some kind of change in the audience. The director is there to help that change occur by making the experience as potent as possible.

Who and what have acted as influences on your work?
I was very struck by the international theatre that I saw in the late seventies and early eighties, in particular the work of Tadeusz Kantor, Pina Bausch, Peter Brook and Ariane Mnouchkine. At the time I thought theatre meant mostly words. Only when I saw companies from Africa and South America, from cultures that had not lost their traditional songs, dances and story-telling methods, did the whole idea of 'a play' begin to change for me.

The cinema has always been a huge inspiration, but of course we are suspicious of its influence, as if all it has bequeathed us are bad playwrights producing short scenes and actors who can't use language – an earthbound, unmagical view of the world. For me one of the most thrilling productions of recent years was Robert Lepage's *The Seven Streams of the River Ota*, with its juxtapositions of time, language and image, its capacity to hurtle us about the world and rush us into the detail of history; it seemed to say, 'Yes, we are a generation that has grown up watching the world through a glass screen: let's celebrate it!' This embracing of technology elevated the theatrical experience rather than reducing it.

Do you feel that you can work as you want in this country?
There aren't many places in this country where one can find the ideal conditions in which to work. Even in a building like the National Theatre questions of product often prevail over process. This is why it is alarming that we keep on putting our money into buildings and not into people. The emphasis on product often forces directors to take a whole series of decisions before the beginning of the actual rehearsal process. I had a particularly painful experience when working on a production of Shakespeare's *Pericles* at the National Theatre (1994–5) where for logistical reasons we had to conceive our set design before the read-through. I had brought together an extraordinary group of people to make this production. The cast came from all sorts of cultural and national backgrounds: some were classically trained actors, some were contemporary dancers, some spoke English with diffidence and some were from a tradition of physical theatre. Over the weeks in the rehearsal room we went on a journey of discovery into the unknown that led us further and

further away from our starting-point. The problem with this was that the further we went, the more the set, which had been conceived beforehand in a room between myself and the designer, seemed to be removed from our needs.

What do you hope to see developing in terms of the director in the future?
The consequences for theatre in this country given the recent years of collapsing subsidy are serious. The whole ecology of theatre has been upset, depriving young directors, actors and designers of the opportunities that were available to my generation.

The debate about whether directors should or could be trained has not got very far, probably because many key players in the directing establishment are not trained. In Britain, training in the theatre has always been very *ad hoc* and spiraling deficits are bound to cancel opportunities that would otherwise be there. My feeling is that you can't give someone an aptitude for theatre, but you can teach them skills: if someone has a gift for singing they would both practise and study with inspirational teachers. In my view, many are defensive of their so called 'process' probably because they don't have one. Directors should talk to each other more, and those of us in a position to do so should take on assistants and trainees.

We are terribly trapped by many of our theatre buildings, which by and large do not contain flexible spaces and thus severely limit our imaginative possibilities. If we are going to create new buildings, let's make ones in which the exploration of the relationship between the audience and the play can be ever changing. Above all, let there be more of a move to fund individuals and their ideas.

Do you think there is such thing as a universal performance language?
The whole world recognizes expressions of sorrow or joy. Yet as soon as sound (music or words) is introduced, potential barriers begin to be erected: one person's lullaby might be another's call to arms.

EWAN MARSHALL

Ewan Marshall was born in Edinburgh in 1960. He trained at Bretton Hall in West Yorkshire from 1981 to 1984, and was Associate Director at Theatre Venture and the London Bubble Theatre Company between 1984 and 1989. His work included a mixture of community theatre and professional productions. Between 1991 and 1997 Marshall was Artistic Director of Graeae Theatre Company, an ensemble of disabled people founded in 1980 by actor Nabil Shabin and Richard Tomlinson. Marshall's productions with Graeae are: *Hound* by Maria Oshodi (1991); *A Kind of Immigrant* by Firdaus Kanga (1992); *Soft Vengeance*, adapted by April De Angelis from Albie Sachs's *Soft Vengeance of a Freedom Fighter* (1993); *Ubu*, adapted by Trevor Lloyd from Alfred Jarry's *Ubu Roi* (1994); *Flesh Fly*, a new adaptation of Ben Jonson's *Volpone*, also by Trevor Lloyd (1995); and *What the Butler Saw* by Joe Orton (1997). Since 1997 he has been Artistic Director of the Dukes Theatre in Lancaster and has directed April de Angelis's *The Life and Times of Fanny Hill* (1997), Frank McGuinness's *Someone Who'll Watch Over Me* (1997) and Suzanne Van Lohuizen's *The Whizz Kid* (1998).

What does the term director mean to you?
A director is somebody who provides a framework and direction for a production or company, and is ultimately responsible for the resulting success or failure of it.

What is your principal medium?
Currently it is the disabled artists I work with.

What is the guiding principle of your directing practice?
An intention and desire to work in an inclusive and collaborative way and to be guided by the material and the people I am working with rather than by personal rigidity or imposition. At the moment I am particularly interested in what I would describe as the exploration of excess.

Could you describe the initial phase of your working method?
Peter Brook's description of his early approach to a play as a 'formless hunch' is the best summation I have read of what often feels like a jumbled and chaotic process.

At the beginning of each project all I have is a mixture of images, thoughts and emotions which spasmodically coalesce into something with a more definite shape. This initial stage of my work always consists of a devising period which takes place as early as possible prior to the rehearsal period and involves the whole creative team. This part of the process is particularly important for my work at Graeae because it allows me to frame my ideas around a shared perspective and the specific physicalities of the members of the company.

How do you work in the rehearsal room?
I try very hard to create an ensemble and encourage and welcome people's ideas. Most of the actors I worked with at Graeae had little experience and no formal training, as drama schools continually ignore disabled students. Consequently the best way to work effectively with the actors was to take their individual capacities into account. I had to be very clear about what I wanted and yet be very flexible at the same time. During the rehearsals one of our main objectives was to find the best way of working together. This could take time but it was often a very rich process as the whole company continually reassessed and developed its group skills.

Most of my directing work has involved the use of commissioned writers whom I try to involve in the rehearsal process. I find the relationship with the writer particularly rewarding and try to keep in open dialogue with them throughout the entire process. It was also very important in my work at Graeae to involve a designer in the production process, and to have a set in rehearsal as early as possible to guarantee its effectiveness and accessibility to the cast and the audience. When we did *Hound* (1991), for example, it was necessary to have a set that would tour easily and work for a cast that included two blind and one partially sighted actor. It was essential that the set became a friendly and known environment as it was the only constant element on a very busy tour. The minute the actors stepped off their twenty by twenty foot space, everything else became alien. So the designer, Sue Mayes, built a structure which allowed her to incorporate accessible tactile features. We laid differing lengths of sash cord under a thin carpet. The sash cord was invisible to the sighted members of the audience, but was easily felt underfoot by the cast; so even during the most complicated movement scenes the actors were always confident of their orientation.

In a sense we used a variety of styles. For instance, our last two shows at Graeae, *Ubu* (1994) and *Flesh Fly* (1995), ran simultaneously in two languages: English and British Sign Language. The latter was usually the first language of our deaf actors and I thought it was important that they used the language they were comfortable with. Equally, it was important that actors whose first language was English did not attempt to use British Sign Language or Sign Supported English when they did not have the relevant support or skill. Part of my task as a director was to amalgamate these different languages, so I attempted to include the British Sign Language interpreter within the action of the play by putting him or her centre stage rather than on a platform at the side of the stage. This prevented me from splitting the focus between the Sign Language and the action and created a greater fluidity.

How would you describe your work with Graeae?
My work at Graeae was the most enjoyable coming together of personal feelings, identity, politics, theatrical discovery and innovation.

Graeae was an important and necessary role model and employer of disabled artists in the last nineteen years, but it would be all too easy for the outside world to think of Graeae simply as a 'container' of disabled artists. So it was essential that we pursued a policy and a working pro-gramme that strived for the highest standards and allowed us to be judged as a theatre company first and foremost. The worthy tag that is often attached to Graeae could easily be a limitation for the company.

With *Ubu* we wanted to depart from the kind of work we were previ-ously commissioned to do, which was more directly related to disability issues. The play is a savage and grotesque satire in which Jarry holds up a mirror to a despicable bourgeois public. There was some debate dur-ing the rehearsals as to whether we were going to score a massive own goal by producing a modern day freak show. Yet we soon discovered that we did have something quite exciting and liberating in our hands, something that played with the very fact that disabled actors are usually asked to play either very positive and worthy characters or clichéd nega-tive roles, such as a villain with an obvious deformity. As a company of disabled people we could subvert these issues. Not all companies could have given the play this edge. When we took it to Berlin one newspaper said that we had achieved an alienation effect that other theatre compa-nies could only dream of.

Our production, *Flesh-Fly*, an adaptation of Ben Jonson's *Volpone*, had a similar history. One of the play's main messages was that moral imper-fection results in physical imperfection, such as Volpone's bastard off-spring: the dwarf, the eunuch and the hermaphrodite. This message is the complete opposite of what Graeae tries to communicate, but it was effective for us to sail close to the wind in order to subvert that central premise while remaining true to Jonson's satire on greed and gullibility. Having Nabil Shabin, who is a wheelchair user, playing Volpone allowed his physicality to add to the text by confusing and ultimately subverting Jonson's attempt to link moral and physical imperfection.

Celia and Madame Would-be were played by the same deaf man using Sign Language. It seemed highly appropriate that these characters were played by a man because they were both archetypes in what is essentially a misogynist piece: the virgin Celia whom the other characters want to rip down from her pedestal, and Madame Would-be, an emasculating pantomime dame figure. The fact that the actor playing these two figures was working in another language, one that is physically expressive and can lend itself to true melodrama, added a layer of alienation that seemed appropriate and illuminating.

With both plays we worked from the tradition of the buffoons, the outsiders who were allowed into town once a year to perform for their lords and masters, and did so with a level of hate and contempt that stemmed from the injustice in their everyday lives. If this aggression ever became overt enough to be noticed their lives would have been in danger. This image has much resonance for disabled people and gives a great bite and unity to our work.

Could you expand on this?
Suppose you have a degree of self-respect, suppose you are good at your job, suppose you are happy and content and suddenly you encounter a group of people who see you in a very different way and essentially attempt to downgrade you by looking at you with pity or condescension. When we were working on *Ubu* I went to Morecambe with Graeae to do some field work, and as we were getting off the coach we were running bets on how long it would take for someone to ask us if we were happy. Of course it took less than five seconds. A traffic warden came up to us, patted one of the actors on the head and said: 'Are you happy?' That day we roused enormous interest in the public because though we obviously were a group of disabled people, we were not being shown around by an able-bodied person: that was bewildering for people who assumed that the disabled cannot act for themselves. It is very useful for us at Graeae to absorb this attitude, which we experience as individuals in our everyday lives, and to use it in our work.

Do you think there is such thing as a universal performance language?
I think there is, though I believe it is unrelated to content and style, but rather has to do with intention and the ability to communicate that intention. I suspect that you could watch theatre anywhere in the world, in any country, in any language, and there would be things that you would understand and like and which would communicate strongly to you. Yet the idea of a universal language sounds like something dangerously absolute and defined rather than a constantly evolving process of discovery. Thinking of Graeae, for example, we attempted to make our theatre increasingly accessible, which was particularly complex as the needs of one impairment group, such as people who are blind, can so easily come into conflict with the needs of another group, such as people who are deaf. To pursue the goal of accessible theatre through an imposition of style on every project would be wrong. Concentrating on form rather than content could cause rigidity and inflexibility – the content is what is exciting in the form and not the other way round.

Has your notion of directing changed over the years?
Working with actors with widely differing physical and sensory impairments constantly forces me to challenge assumptions, abandon methods used in the past and pursue specific and relevant ways of working with actors both as individuals and as a company. Quite a few people have commented on this specific way of working in relation to *Ubu*, which was a pastiche of different forms and genres. The actors looked stylistically different. In a sense it is my job to channel the vitality of these different styles towards some kind of cohesion. This individualistic way of working with actors is something I would now pursue with any actor or company, regardless of disability.

How does awareness of audience affect your work?
I've always thought a great deal about audience and I can't imagine not doing so. There is no theatre without audience interaction. The idea of the audience has tremendous influence during the whole process of rehearsals. I am constantly in dialogue with my audience.

At Graeae we worked in a rather rare environment in that we were all disabled people with a shared perspective that can lead to a form of shorthand in the development and understanding of our work. As we went further and further in a certain direction, we had to be careful not to leave substantial sections of our audiences behind by not supplying the necessary steps for them to be able to follow us on our journey.

I found that most audiences were as sophisticated as we were effective, although sometimes we went on stage and experienced a huge shock of non-acceptance. For instance, when we went to the Traverse Theatre with *Ubu* someone came up to me after the show and said, 'Well, one of the actors is disabled, but all the others are pretending, aren't they?' Now the question is: why did this go through that person's head? I think it's because many people just don't see disability around them and so even in the theatre they have an absolute denial when they are confronted with it.

Who and what have acted as influences on your work?
When I became disabled at the age of eighteen I wanted to be an actor, but I was told I had no chance; the only job I was offered was as a radio operator for the police! By chance, I saw Graeae on television in an Arena Documentary broadcast in 1981 which made me realize there might possibly be a life outside the police force. In particular I was impressed and inspired by the power and talent of Nabil Shabin.

The writings of Peter Brook and Antonin Artaud have also been a great influence. There is something beautifully accessible and inspiring about the writings of Peter Brook: what he says is deceptively simple and yet enormously powerful. Reading Artaud's work is like being wired up to the mains. I never fully comprehend what he is trying to say, but so much of it makes me want to rush out and start doing things. Cicely Berry, the voice coach who works with the Royal Shakespeare Company, is the best teacher I have ever watched or worked with.

How do you see yourself in terms of the European theatrical landscape?
Graeae has been in existence for nineteen years. Nabil Shabin and Richard Tomlinson founded it from desire but also total need. Although Nabil is a very good actor, he did not get an entrance interview from a single drama school or college in the country. To a certain extent this situation has not changed: the disabled are still being denied work in the theatre or in drama schools because those who run them believe their aspirations to be unrealistic. This leads to a vicious circle: many disabled actors are not considered good enough by employers because they are not trained, and drama colleges think: what is the point in training them if they'll never get a job because they've had no training? This cycle needs breaking.

When I think of other groups that are formed around need and oppression, the disabled often seem to be last on the list. It's still very difficult to persuade reviewers to come and see our work. Those who do review our work often start with: 'This sounded so unpromising as an evening' or 'I came here thinking that I'd have to be a little patronizing'. Some of our work tries to be directly confrontational of these issues. I think Graeae has an extremely significant role to play: it is unique as a theatre company for disabled people who are pursuing drama and theatre as art rather than therapy. Of course there is a place for therapy, but there should be no confusion between that and Graeae's work.

When we took *Soft Vengeance* to Minsk (1993) the only theatre we saw which was run by disabled people was in a hospital. We were treated with nervousness until we started working in the theatre, and then suddenly there was the realization that we had a lot in common as theatre practitioners. The visit became a truly memorable exchange.

We can never forget how disabled people are treated in all societies. This is also why we must never forget that we are involved in a human rights struggle: our theatre is the contribution to that struggle.

Do you feel you can work as you want to work in this country?
No, but I would be very surprised if anyone could answer that question positively. I think it is scandalous that Graeae has been playing for nineteen years and still receives such scanty funding. The funding bodies should be aware that they are helping something to develop which is unique in this country and represents a potential role model, maybe even for other countries. The funding bodies and other institutions need to open their doors to disabled performers and artists in order to start harnessing the enormous talent that is there.

What would you hope to see developing in terms of the director and their role in the next few years?
It is good to see the start of an attempt to address the lack of training for directors. I also think that it will be important to look at what the excessive financial cuts over the last decade have done to individual directors' perceptions of what they can achieve and how they work best. The fact that so many directors spend a huge amount of their time trying to defend their theatres against more cuts is very damaging. Obviously, I hope that disabled people will be represented in future theatre.

SIMON McBURNEY

Simon McBurney, an actor and writer, was born in Cambridge in 1957. He studied English at Cambridge University and trained at the Jacques Lecoq school in Paris. In 1982 he co-founded Theatre de Complicite with Annabel Arden and Marcello Magni; he is Artistic Director of the company. His work with Complicite includes: *Put It On Your Head* (1983), *A Minute Too Late* (1984), *More Bigger Snacks Now* (1985), *FoodStuff* (1986), *Please Please Please* (1986), *Alice in Wonderland* (1987), *Anything for a Quiet Life* (1987), *The Visit* (1989, Almeida, Royal National Theatre, Riverside Studios), *My Army Parts One and Two* (1989), *The Winter's Tale* (1992), *The Street of Crocodiles* (1992-4, Royal National Theatre and West End), *The Three Lives of Lucie Cabrol* (1994), *Out of a House Walked a Man* (1994, co-production with the Royal National Theatre) and *The Caucasian Chalk Circle* (1997, Royal National Theatre).

What is your starting-point as a director?

The *sensation* is that I start with nothing because nothing exists. The beginning, the origin of a piece of theatre is never clear, even if it is an established play, because the play consists of words on a page and this in itself does not qualify those words as theatre. The words may appear to be something substantial in themselves, but they are not. How many times have I been to a performance of a Shakespeare play and had the feeling that the play itself was not good because the theatre wasn't good? There is a curious and very different sensation when you apparently have something in your hands – a play – and when you have nothing but fragments, scraps and imaginings when you are devising; yet strangely I feel I start from the same place: until I start to feel and experience something, there is nothing.

I often ask myself what the origin is for doing a piece and I have to conclude that there is no origin: if you start looking for a single point of departure you will never find it – as historians we all impose a neat structure on the past. One of the things I find interesting about the beginning of a piece is what pushed my desire in the first place; I'll have an impulse and during rehearsals I'll go miles and miles away from it only to return to it, to revisit and refind the point of departure.

The beginning of a piece is something to do with our relationship with time, and this is one of the principal concerns in my work. The beginning is always now. I'm not being deliberately obscure when I say this, I'm always struck by how a piece of theatre varies from night to night, and by how much it is made anew. That crucial percentage of difference has an enormous impact in the minds of the audience. I've made pieces that I've imagined would be continually successful and then suddenly I find that they don't function as I thought they would. So the beginning of a piece invokes an incredible tentativeness within me. The ideas that I originally had disappear once work begins. I think I have to say that the work itself is the beginning; it's only when you 'do' that imaginings become reality. Many directors work out everything in advance, and this kind of theatre is constricted by a straitjacket of ideas and concepts, having no natural relationship to itself, no natural growth.

What do you mean by 'natural growth'?
When I started working on the Daniel Kharms's piece *Out of a House Walked a Man* (1994) no one could believe that I didn't have a script. Where you begin is where you try to prepare the ground, and for three weeks I prepared people. One morning I put half an hour of the show together in fifteen minutes. This could not have happened unless people's reservoirs had been filled, unless those people had found out what they had in common. What filled the reservoir was a 'common language', and what these people had in common was an 'openness' which allows for growth and development. This is what I mean by 'natural' and what the 'preparation' was about. At this point it is also important to make a clear distinction between what is 'natural' and the style of naturalism. Naturalism is a style in the way that melodrama and *commedia dell'arte* are styles: they are points of arrival and closure, not points of departure. I am talking about the process that happens before the imposition of style.

If you cultivate a garden and you plant too many things in it before you have given it a chance to breathe, the garden will become choked up and will never achieve its own life. The classical Augustan ideas that you can impose an order on nature and that nature will bend to the human will have disappeared. There is disillusion with the Romantic ideals. We live in times of an unbelievable desire for certainty generated by the notion of the economic free market. In our desire for economic certainties we have lost the sense of time or space to allow for uncertainties.

It's not for nothing that people in theatre work for years with the same collaborators. In this sense the beginning is very important; it is a problematic situation in theatre today because we've taken away the centre of theatre – we come at it attempting to predict the outcome. Thus a producer has an idea and goes to a director and designer, who help to shape it, then they find an actor and they fill in the rest of the company around that actor. I'm not saying that this system can't work, but on the whole it squeezes the lifeblood out of the theatre and it works against the natural origins of a piece. In this system the writer has a strange satellite position in the work. Often the writer is not the start-ing-point, and when the writer is brought in he or she is curiously disas-sociated from the work because everyone assumes that their work is finished once rehearsals start. There can also be an over-reverence for a text, when people argue that the script is a bible and cannot be diverged from in any way. The structure of work which appears more natural to me is to begin by acknowledging that the company of actors has a life of its own which cannot be denied, unless you are a life-denying director. It is the uncertainty which brings life, which, of course, is why you work for a long time with the same collaborators. Only through the establish-ment of trust can you venture into uncertainty.

If you start from the company of actors together with the script, you admit that whatever the piece is, it is a combination of things and does not come about through the exclusion of one or the other. It is right that the director enables this growth to take place. The designer tills the ground and landscapes it accordingly, and finally the producer enables this piece to be put on. I don't want to be misunderstood on this point. I'm talking about the acknowledgement of priorities; a belief in the source of something which needs to be nurtured into life rather than pollarded into a stunted and forced shape.

I'm fascinated by this notion of the origin of a piece of work. In 1981 Neil Bartlett and I made a piece of street theatre called *Beach Buoys*. Ini-tially he wrote to me and said that he had an image of delicately painted clowns playing in the faded resorts of the south coast: that's one origin. But the year before he'd come to see me in Paris when I'd been working with a teacher of clowns: this is another origin. In 1980 we saw each other's work in Edinburgh and spent a day talking to find out what we had in common, and on that day our mutual delight in the gravestones of Greyfriars cemetery could be seen as a third point of departure. The fourth origin lay in our rehearsals, for which we had few ideas at first but laughed ourselves to the point of collapse. Each of these are points of origin, but I like to think that the combination of observation (the grave-yard), preparation (the teaching), proposition (the letter) and action (the rehearsals) were the combination of events needed for any piece of theatre to achieve its aim. I believe that we instinctively followed the right journey. At any rate it culminated in us fronting the rock group Bauhaus at the Hammersmith Odeon before an audience of three thousand and it was one of the most remarkable evenings in my life.

Where do you think theatre comes from?
Gordon Craig said that 'Dance is the parent of theatre.' I've tried to reflect on what he meant by that. The why of the theatre has preoccu-pied me more as I have got older. Intellectually I become increasingly interested in that 'why', and I think it connects with my father's work as an archaeologist and his concern with origins.

I see dance as a kind of celebration, as an excess of emotion when rhythms are beaten out in some way. It is to do with an internal journey being expressed in physical action/movement; as that action finds form you arrive at style, at a framework for the dance; the rhythm gradually becomes associated with music, and the music becomes specific and is formed into sounds and words, then it becomes theatre.

Perhaps this is what Craig meant by 'Dance is the parent of theatre.' When you dance together you have a form which represents the collec-tive imagination; it expresses what we feel together at a particular moment. If theatre is to have power it is when it manages to touch on what is a primal and universal human need. Words emanate from a physical act in the body, and for me the body is where you begin in the rehearsal room.

How do you begin work with your performers?
The encounter on the first day is always strange. The beginning is a very secret moment, I think. There is no formula for it. If I sense that people are embarrassed then I might do something really ridiculous to relax them; if they're over-relaxed then I might do something to give them a jolt; if they're tense I try to relieve their anxiety. I get people up on their feet immediately. I do this not only to begin moving the body but also to make the actors come at the subject obliquely. The sudden surprise of discovery can often reveal much more about a text, for exam-ple, than approaching it directly. I'm not saying this is the answer, but the process is not always helped by sitting around reading. Of course you have to stop and think about what you're doing, but ultimately

there is only the doing on stage. I try to discover what the dynamic in the room is, so I start with the people in the room and try to be as open as possible to what they propose. I am well prepared for rehearsals, but it is important to do unexpected things and I am ready to change my plans at any point.

Peter Brook invited me to a workshop a few years ago with a number of other directors. He wanted to know which of us began the day with the physical preparation of our actors. It was difficult for most of us in that workshop to understand the value of this. The value in preparation, other than facilitating greater communication between people, is again to do with the unexpected. I do not prepare people so that they know more about where they are going. I prepare them so that they are ready: ready to change, ready to be surprised, ready to seize any opportunity that comes their way. The great paradox for a director is that one feels, or perhaps the expectation demands, that one comes up with an answer. This is also my difficulty with interviews: I have no answers at all. There are no formulae. I suppose I can understand why people rely on read-throughs and fixed models of working: we're all terrified of what we don't know, aghast at the idea of uncertainty. Our faith in priests has been betrayed and so we placed it in economists, and recently that's been wearing thin. Perhaps we don't know where to put our faith now, but beginning a piece with faith is important.

Peter Brook has said that there are two questions that a director needs to ask themselves throughout their working life. These are: why am I doing theatre? and how can I make theatre? What do you think about this?
I think the answer lies in the moment of collective imagining. For a moment you hold up a rope, then stretch it out on the floor and then walk across it pretending to be on a tightrope, and somehow people will go along with you: they won't believe you are on a tightrope but they will accept the story. In *A Minute too Late* (1984) we represented grave-stones with any old bricks in the street, but people transported themselves to a cemetery. In *Street of Crocodiles* (1992–4) books transformed into birds, school desks changed shape, a piece of cloth suddenly became magical because of the way it was touched. Only theatre can do this, only theatre has this particularity of time. The act of collective imagining creates a bond between us which links us to the same society and the same sense of being; it confirms something very particular about the communication between us. The need for this affirmation is common to all societies, though, of course, forms differ.

Why do I make theatre? It's not a dominant art form in the twentieth century and architecturally you can even chart the rise of theatre in the nineteenth century and its decline in the twentieth. One starts from a position of marginalization in theatre. At the same time theatre has ritual functions in society and it is associated with signs of cultural health and economic strength, but a theatre that is *living* is marginalized, gasps for breath and appears to be dying. Of course, it won't die when there are people who are passionate about it, but finding its life is still difficult. Enormous numbers of people go to see theatre despite the fact that much of it is a strange relic. I think most people would not admit that theatre is essential in their lives. That's why I would suggest we need theatre. If we don't have it we create it. A great aspect of medieval theatre were the processions, and commentators remarked on the piteous beauty of the poor and dispossessed processing through the streets. This kind of theatre is a form of community theatre and is still very present. It is a collective ritual theatre of celebration and we need it. I link this form of theatre to sporting occasions which play a similar role in our society.

Why am I doing theatre? How can I make theatre? I don't know if I have answered these questions or whether they are truly answerable. The interesting point is that Brook dares to ask these things. Brook asks questions; he also creates and searches for a theatre that is 'alive'. There is a connection, and it is that there is tremendous energy in a question – even in the movement of the body, the eyes search, the head turns and the hands open up. When we demand a hard and fast definition the answer lies on the ground like a piece of concrete; what was imaginative possibility becomes banal reality.

You've talked about your fascination with time. Could you elaborate on that?
Theatre has a relationship with time that no other art form has, in that it exists in the *present*, and human beings have a need to be present in this life. There is a great deal around us that appears to bring us into contact with the present, but in fact we tend to live in the recent past or the immediate future. I have always found it interesting that one of Complicite's most successful early comedies took the theme of the present to its idiotic extreme. It was a piece about maximum satisfaction called *More Bigger Snacks Now* (1985), which revolved around having nothing, but dreaming of better things.

Theatre is unique in that everything happens in the present, and I think that the only way theatre can develop is to increase its acknowledgement of the present moment instead of emulating television. The vogue of naturalistic issue-based writing since the sixties speaks for itself: people try to bring real issues to the stage, and the problem with that is that television will always do it so much better. Ultimately on the stage you'll always see that the door wobbles when someone closes it, or the theatre lantern gives out. Theatre can only exist if all these elements are celebrated as an integral part of it, not focused on as shortcomings.

We tend to be preoccupied with what we will have next, and that is linked to exchange of money and our obsession with materiality: there is no end to this mountain of money we wish to accumulate. This has led to a desire to spend less and less time on things: we don't want to have to seek out a telephone so we have mobile telephones and as a result move further away from the present. The present is now measured in milliseconds.

What are your thoughts on audience?
Audience and the acknowledgement of audience are fundamental to me: there has to be that thread of companionship. When we did *The Winter's Tale* (1992) Annie Castledine was incredibly helpful in focusing the way we spoke the soliloquies: we didn't speak them to thin air but directly to the audience. That acknowledgement of audience has to happen all the time. When something supposedly 'goes wrong' in the performance, far from ruining the atmosphere it makes the whole experience so much more intense. I remember in Friedrich Dürrenmatt's play *The Visit* (1991) two giant tables fell over and the whole cast rallied round to reposition them. The audience knew that we were improvising but they didn't drop their suspension of disbelief. On another occasion Kathryn Hunter fainted and we stopped the show for ten minutes while she recovered. I then retold the story to the audience in one and a half minutes. The electricity in the audience in both these instances was much greater and audience attention was heightened. The sense of the present became palpable and the audience were made much more aware that anything might go wrong or change at any given moment. On these occasions the applause we received had a quite different quality to it than is usual: the audience realized that they had a complicit participation in a creative act.

Historically styles have developed in the theatre that have placed more distance between the audience and the performance. For example, *commedia dell'arte* street theatre influenced theatre across Europe, including Shakespeare. But later it was appropriated by Goldoni who turned what was a popular working-class form into a bourgeois art form. You can trace how that style became even more heightened in the nineteenth century through people like Puccini. One of the problems in the twentieth century has been the death of popular theatre: variety and music hall have been swallowed up by television, which has nothing of the 'presence' of theatre. So theatre has become a place for middle-class intellectuals. Theatre has to re-seize its language, its theatricality.

What do you feel you are doing as a director?
In the early shows I think we created circumstances in which we were able to imagine and create. In *A Minute too Late* (1984) every aspect was geared to opening our imaginations and amusing ourselves so that we could be as creative as possible. We made ourselves writers as well as actors.

When I direct I come from the viewpoint of an actor, and everything I do is linked to releasing the creativity of the actor. I want them to understand the form of what they are doing; if they're acting in a play I want them to understand the themes. I want them to hold the piece in their hands; but that understanding is not an intellectual process, it is a physical one, they have to *feel* it.

With *Street of Crocodiles* I had a strong feeling towards the book and I knew the kind of story I wanted to tell. The stories themselves were merely fragments, and it became clear that narrative structure would not be the thing that would hold the piece together; it was something closer to a fugue and variations. I constantly had to invent circum-stances, games and environments where actors would see what they were doing but still be happy to spiral off creatively. I developed a whole language of transformation with them, a language which enabled them to control the imaginative leap from one medium to another. People talked of the choreography, but it wasn't choreographed; instead, through innumerable improvisations the actors physically learned to shift together, like a flock of starlings. They learned to dip and wheel and found a fantastic pleasure in it. This required enormous physical discipline and they worked extremely hard every day; it is this discipline of body and voice that is fundamental in my work.

Are there preoccupations that reoccur in your work?
It's too easy to create a historical pattern for your work. I work instinc-tively and then see that there is a formal shape to a piece that I didn't expect.

SIMON MCBURNEY

Are you aware of influences on your work?
As a child I grew up with pantomime – Cyril Fletcher was a great favourite of mine. Someone called Enid Welsford lived next door; she loved *commedia dell'arte* and wrote a book called *The Fool* and she had quite an influence on me. I grew up without television; my mother wrote us plays and we performed them – I loved that. From an early age I was aware of what bored me in theatre. In the 1970s there were a great number of shows from abroad in England and I watched what Peter Gill and David Gothard brought to the Riverside Studios. I remember the Indian Naya theatre with Habib Tanvir. I worked with Dario Fo. In Paris I saw the work of Mnouchkine, Philippe Avron and Besson. I remember the music theatre of a Dutch group called Die Mexicanshund and the Belgian clowning company Radaeus. I'd go and see anything. There was a sense of enormous freedom, as though things could go in any direction. It was a climate of imagination and creativity which was not bound by economic success and that rubbed off on me.

It was never my intention to become a director; I've always been an actor. It's painful being a director and people have flattered me into the role: I don't feel I have control in the sense of knowing and planning where I'm going. I don't know what I'm doing next. I always experience an enormous release of creativity when I'm performing myself. I've always had a hand in directing the shows for Complicite; my input has involved giving a direction. But working with the same people time and again has been very important; theatre is a collaborative process and I would stress that all the actors and artists we have worked with over the years have been integral to what has emerged. I knew the kind of theatre I was interested in and wanted. It gradually evolved that I would some-times stand on the outside, though I much prefer to be on the inside as well as the outside.

Could you talk more about the theatre language you develop amongst the actors?
I am adamant about unifying people through a common language. Parameters of communication are essential in the rehearsal room. You can't make assumptions. Once you've built up a common language you can work very fast. By language I mean a physical, vocal, musical and architectural language: all those elements which make up a theatre lan-guage. Sometimes I leave the actors to prepare something which we then look at; it can be tremendously liberating for actors to work with-out the director. What matters is that when you say something, the

other person understands; I mean understanding unconsciously as well as consciously. I do a lot of work in the area of the unconscious: we might play children's games, or paint all morning, or work with clay; we might work with buckets of water, or create instruments out of pots and pans. In all this the object is to exercise different muscles. We might sing all day, blindfold one another and listen to each others' voices, but this work is always linked to the central aim of increasing awareness and communication. The theatre language you move towards is not a constant one, it is defined by the material in front of you. Hence the quality of the communication between the actors directly helps the evaluation of whether the choices you make on a given piece are appropriate or not. I would like to stress again that there is not one single theatre language or, worse still, a single Theatre de Complicite language which we move towards; there is only the development of tact, that is, an ability to make the right choice from a myriad of possibilities.

Another myth I would like to explode are the physical capabilities attributed to the company. Sometimes people say to us, 'You must be so fit!', 'You're so supple, so co-ordinated!' Ah, what a pleasure to be flattered! How important to hide the truth! In real life many of us are unco-ordinated, stiff and overweight. Theatre is not how you *are* in real life, but the quality of the illusion you can create on stage. The stiffest actors, if they are good actors, can convey the most astonishing sense of suppleness.

Can you work as you want to in this country?
We don't work only in this country; we come from several countries and we work in several countries. Wherever you end up there is always this problem of space as well as time and money; after twelve years Complicite are still looking for rehearsal space in London. But I don't want to blame the circumstances of my work if something goes wrong with a piece. Sometimes I try not to think about it. In the past I made work by hook or by crook. Sometimes we made very good work in hideous circumstances. Sometimes it's right to do a piece in three weeks; at other times you feel you need twelve months. Sometimes it can be beneficial if circumstances are not as you desire them to be; this creates an energy of resistance and a determination to bring something to life in a deathless landscape.

There are moments when the sheer tyranny of the lack of resources stifles the spirit. Many times in the past five years I've felt that I couldn't go on. Nevertheless there are times when I'm happy to make something out of nothing; it's an ethos I grew up with. In a show with few objects and a simple design you have them in the rehearsal room from day one, but when you have more and larger elements such as in *Out of a House Walked a Man*, the convention is that you get them late in the process and inevitably they don't function as you thought they would. It is important that everything you wish to play with in the performance is present during the creative process, otherwise it's impossible to make it live when you get on to the stage. For me the objects I use are like words on a page; the rules of their movement are like grammar and syntax. The way they are integrated makes them articulate; their eloquence lies in the respect with which you touch them. Their stillness highlights their movement, just as silence underpins poetry. The circumstances of your work must, therefore, coincide with the respect with which you treat your art. When I worked in Japan I was struck by how the actors treated their working space; not only were their shoes left at the door, but there was also a place to put yourself in the room. We do not have these reflexes in England. Equally we do not have a powerful and ancient theatre tradition. We have to invent our own circumstances, as we have now to reinvent our theatre.

CLIFFORD McLUCAS AND MIKE PEARSON

Clifford McLucas was born in Yorkshire and read Architecture at Manchester University during the 1960s. He moved to Wales in the seventies and began collaborating with Brith Gof (a Welsh idiom for 'faint recollection') in the 1980s, eventually becoming a full-time company member in 1988. He is now joint Artistic Director with Mike Pearson and has been key to the company's large-scale site-specific projects since 1989. He has also been responsible for Brith Gof's television productions over recent years and continues to be preoccupied with Brith Gof's practice and presence across a range of cultural forms and media. Currently, he is engaged in a three-year programme of work in West Wales, prosiectecs, that integrates performance, landscape, architecture and multimedia.

Mike Pearson was born in Lincolnshire and read Archaeology at Cardiff in the late 1960s. He received an MA from the University of Wales for a thesis on the work of community arts groups such as Inter-Action. He was a founder member of RAT Theatre, and amongst the earliest practitioners of physical theatre in Britain, working with Cardiff Laboratory Theatre which established close ties with Eugenio Barba's Odin Teatret. In 1980 he studied Noh in Tokyo with Kanze Hideo and learned Welsh. He has been co-director of Brith Gof since its foundation in 1981. In a recent series of publications and practical projects, he has been examining points of convergence between performance and archaeology. Currently, he is Lecturer in Performance Studies at the Department of Film, Television and Theatre Studies, University of Wales Aberystwyth.

What do you understand by theatre and directing?

CLIFFORD MCLUCAS: I suppose I understand theatre as making composite art. I have a difficulty with this word 'director'. What is it? Is it a role spread between several people, or is it one 'legitimate' overseer? When Brith Gof started out there were four of us with varying skills: architecture, music, text, physical performance. The centre of Mike's practice is physical performance work; the centre of mine is architecture.

MIKE PEARSON: We work in the field of 'devised performance'. This does not entail getting a group of people together and saying, 'What shall we make?' From the outset we begin with a series of conceptual practices, which involve place and performance. We generate theatrical material in all four axes of its manifestation: space, time, pattern and detail. For us the directorial process is not simply one of animating or illustrating textual material.

I think performance may be manifest as choreography, as dramaturgy or as art. These three all have very different operating principles; that's not to say that all three can't be present in any one performance, but I come from the old tradition of physical theatre and I'd say that I work in dramaturgy – the notions that arose in physical theatre in the 1980s were to do with choreography.

You talked of the four axes in theatre: what are 'pattern' and 'detail'?
MP: I mean dramaturgical pattern and detail. By pattern I mean the scenario: the plan or series of events, narratives, occurrences – singly or in parallel. Detail refers to textual or gestural detail, in any one of a number of preferred media.

How do you work together?
CM: I'm not a performer. Mike performs in some of the pieces, often in solos. Mike thinks about the work in terms of its physical performance. I think about the work in terms of architectures – not literally buildings, though that can be relevant because we do a large proportion of site-specific work – but the internal ligaments and structures that hold a piece together. I spend a great deal of time on that kind of conceptual process before we actually start working with performers. The having of an idea, the setting of the internal architecture of that idea, the research of the material, the writing of texts, the authoring of a piece of work – if all this comes under 'directing', then that's what we do. Our notion of directing a piece of work is very broad; it involves a whole scheme of things, a whole series of processes from the having of an idea.

Could you elaborate on those processes?
CM: They vary from production to production. One of the things that we decided recently is that either Mike or I should be the producer of a piece. For *Tri Bywyd* or *Three Lives* (1995) I am the producer, which means I shape up the production, organize funding, staging and when and where it is performed. Then we reach the point of working the material itself, writing texts, designing lighting and sets, and we each have specific roles. On the other hand, Mike's solo show *From Memory* (1991) didn't involve me at all: he wrote, researched and performed it himself. The models we operate are broad.

What are your methods of research?

CM: I'll talk about this in relation to our piece *Y Pen Bas/Y Pen Dwfn* or *The Shallow End/The Deep End* (1995). Often for me an initial stimulation for a piece will be a place. For a long time I was interested in doing something in a swimming pool. The very particular environment interested me as an architect: the visual aspects, the fact that water surfaces can be languid or animated, the singular acoustics. There are two worlds: one underwater and one above. I was curious to know what that might mean for performers. How would it be possible to operate in these two worlds? One world has air, the other no air. The performers had to cope with the environment they were in; this is a running preoccupation in our work. This makes things real; if someone is running about in a downpour they get cold and wet, they don't have to pretend. The physical performance in our work is real and the audience picks up on this.

Eventually I chose to do the piece specifically around the flooding of a valley in northern Wales in the 1950s and 1960s, which was done to create a reservoir for Liverpool. Within that axis there was a wealth of political, social and cultural material to be mined; the research took me a year. It eventually became a project about the 'colonial' relationship between Wales and England. In order to avoid the material merely being about a historical set of events, I incorporated aspects of Daniel Defoe's *Robinson Crusoe* into the piece. The research involved TV programmes, reading, interviews. We're talking boxes and boxes of research. That gives rise to a very, very detailed scenario. We often produce a storyboard for a project rather than a script – any text might be on a soundtrack. Much that we use is pre-existing material that we haven't written – radio archives, perhaps; we're drawn to that kind of material because the grain of reality comes with it.

We come back to certain material again and again over the years. We always do the research ourselves; it's part of the process of creating this composite art. We often use bodies of material that co-exist in our pieces: historical material, personal textual material, analytical material. I'm always surprised that others don't work like this.

MP: During the build-up to a piece we are imagining how known performers might function in certain circumstances, so 'directing' is part of this conceptual process. Pressures at the site vary because of all the media involved; it may even be that the particular conditions we want to create for the performers may not be 'available' until very close to the performance indeed. That means I go through a process of 'imagining' with the performers. For example, one of our projects, *Haearn* or *Iron* (1992), combined the narratives of Frankenstein, the myth of Prometheus, the decline of the steel industry and medical experiments in the eighteenth century. One of the performers was hooked on to a transporter crane that travelled the full length of the building. He was in a swivel harness that allowed him to cartwheel and blow fire at the same time. The conditions for actual rehearsal were only available for three days before the performance when we got the crane. He spent three weeks hanging off a static rope creating the right mental conditions for his performance. It was remarkable!

How do you work with your performers?
MP: Whilst I can't exactly put my finger on it, I think there is a Brith Gof style of performance which is something to do with the application of time and energy – more or less – in a performer's work as opposed to everyday life. We do a lot of 'ganging'; any theatre exists not just as a work group but as a social group as well. One has to create a team – it's more akin to sport than theatre; everyone knows their specific function, but they also know how they relate to the team as a whole.

I have to get my performers' confidence. I wouldn't ask them to do anything I wouldn't do myself. I once saw one of Eugenio Barba's performers get his hand stuck in a rope: Barba was the first person up there, helping him. I never, never have an 'emperor's seat'. There's never a fixed locale in the rehearsal room from where we look at the work; I'm always looking at it in 3D to see how the performers function.

Could you elaborate on your directing practice?
MP: I've started developing work that is simultaneous, work where there may be several activities going on in one area simultaneously. There might be a standing audience, a sitting audience, or both; it might be a moving audience. In this sense one is directing in a musical way, trying to make sure that a meaning is emerging from the conducting of material and audience.

CM: It's a symphonic model; a question of trying to get the parts to work together, to resonate. You might not be able to pin the meaning down. For *Tri Bywyd*, which we're staging in a forest, we bring together three narratives; they resonate with and against each other and become more than the sum of their parts. Our theatre is constructed by bringing things together which pre-exist, and bringing this symphonic relationship to them. This is always what we do, even in Mike's solos. So the notion of the director as being at the middle of some point, or the pinnacle of a mountain doesn't mean anything to us; it never feels like that.

MP: It's complex. The nature of the information and the medium which carries it can change from second to second. Directing the performers is an awkward business: they may not be the most important thing going on in any one moment. Conventionally, everyone looks at the performers: they carry the narrative, they mediate and alter it. In our big pieces the performers can't do this. Any one member of the audience may register a detail to the exclusion of something else. For us the performers are only one level of the performance, and that's unusual; but directing includes a constant process of reinforcing what the performers are doing.

We create 'maps' so that the performers can orientate themselves. Very often one of those maps is a time map; they might work in patterns of set time, say ten sections of six minutes each. They might fall into silences during that time but they have to understand what patterns of six minutes are. Generally we know the emotional flavour of each section, though the components don't come together until the last minute.

CM: Everyone but Mike and I works blind during that time – we know where we want to go but it's sometimes frightening. You've been imagining it for three months and you suddenly discover that twenty ton cranes go at half the speed you thought!

MP: I regret that rehearsal periods are no longer than in conventional theatre – three weeks. We institute *études* which are performances we put in front of people that allow us to experiment with a particular soundtrack, technology or physicality prior to its inclusion in large-scale work. It's very difficult to say if there are rules of engagement. The process is fluid. There's no template; we change and develop.

I suppose I tend towards *bricolage*. Directing is often seen as a process akin to science; of analysis and synthesis. The director starts with the question: 'What do I want and how do I get there?' As a *bricoleur* I ask: 'What have I got lying around to build a performance with?' The stuff lying around is the materials, the personalities and abilities of the performers. The performers help to contribute to and define what the thing is through their abilities much more than conventional theatre allows. The performers are much more *implicated* in what the material is and how it has arisen.

Could you talk about your work in relation to Wales?

CM: We do this kind of work because we're based in Wales, and there are all kinds of traditions here which do not exist elsewhere. Brith Gof has taken on the shape it has through the interface between personal desires, personal artistic ambitions and the reality of where we live.

We rarely perform in theatres: one of the reasons is that the Welsh-speaking community may see them as 'colonial outposts', and it's the Welsh-speaking community that we're committed to. Also it might be that in making a particular piece for a particular community a theatre building would be the last thing you'd think of. It's to do with the relationship between England and Wales; there's a strong tendency from a dominated culture to accept the dominant culture as a given. Hence the controversy surrounding the possibility of a Welsh National Theatre.

We're very advanced in terms of our engagement with the site and its ability to activate a particular culture. Our work is about place and audience – this isn't a neutral set of people who come along and sit in the dark. I suppose our audience is like a constituency and that's why Brith Gof's work has developed as very implicated work within Wales. We do site-specific work because we're in Wales – that's the nearest to the truth I can get.

MP: We're concerned with notions of authenticity, inauthenticity and hybridity. We draw on whatever theatrical conventions are appropriate. We aren't afraid to hybridize music and text in a way which doesn't resemble a musical. We can do a Noh play in Welsh. There's always a musical soundtrack in our work.

CM: This word 'hybrid' is important. It's natural for us, the whole of Wales hybridizes itself. There's a very fractured culture between the Welsh and non-Welsh speakers, and an endless re-negotiation and hybridization of identity. Models in England are much less questioned. In Wales sitting in a black box looking at a hole in the wall may be an odd thing to do.

There's no great tradition of dramatic literature in Wales. There aren't the models, and as a result theatre practice in Wales is disparate and diverse. There's more of a collision between the personal and the political.

I'd say there's been a comparatively recent cultural relaxation due to a new Welsh presence in Europe. Wales is bilingual like most European countries. We're innovative and contemporary in this sense.

Do you believe in a universal language in theatre?

MP: No. It's a notion that worries me a lot and it's a very dominant notion in England. What always fascinates me is the strangeness about something, the oddness. It's when I see a performance and think: I don't really know what's happening here – that's when I get excited. All of us run into tremendous problems with this presumption of a universal language. It's happened to us at the Royal Court Theatre: we dared to speak Welsh, and it was a high-level offence, a strangeness that critics couldn't cope with.

CM: The dominant concern in orthodox theatre is to produce something that is like a well-formed, perfect object, a piece of sculpture. But everything we do is about hybridization, about internal fractures within work, bodies of material that co-exist rather than unify. The piece we took to the Royal Court, *Patagonia* (1992), was to do with the deconstructed identities of the Welsh people, about fractured meanings. These are strange things to the theatre establishment. The worse thing we could do is make a well-rounded object from this material, but there isn't a preparedness amongst conventional theatre to come face to face with work like this. I find that astonishing and sad.

Could you talk about your audiences?

CM: You're right, we do have audiences in the plural. They are not fixed and forever and there's a constant dynamic in our relationship to them.

We are incredibly aware of our constituencies and much of our work is bilingual, though we try to create performances which are not simultaneously translating themselves; to create at least two separate narratives and bodies of information flowing in different languages. This means that the English-speakers are not excluded and perhaps hear the Welsh as a white noise; for the Welsh-speaker it mirrors their day-to-day existence. There's a negotiation between two languages which perhaps bemuses, shocks or interests. We become more and more interested in the choices we make in saying something in Welsh or English and the different cultural resonances that can lie behind a piece of text.

We did a piece in Cardiff called *Arturius Rex* (1994) and we sensed that there was a new group of people coming to see our work: young Welsh speakers without the traditions of older generations. We're now developing a model for our next project, *Prydain* or *The Impossibility of Britishness*, which is directly in response to our perception of the shift in

(84)

audience. Is there a model for a different kind of musical experience in theatre, for a rave? We think about such things all the time. The question isn't as simple as: how do we communicate with our audiences? It's how do we set up a dialogue, an engagement between the event and the audience?

MP: In a small nation you can go to work with ideas and events which have a more common currency than in a majority culture. You can work with ideas that you'll know almost everyone in the audience will have a grip on, an attitude towards. We choose content that has a place within the discourses in Wales. For example, *Y Pen Bas/Y Pen Dwfn* that I mentioned before was about a subject that still outrages the Welsh even today, but when I interviewed the chairman of the water company in Liverpool, who was responsible for flooding the valley, he had all but forgotten the enterprise. That was material that had different cultural appreciations.

I feel it is culturally irresponsible to take something at face value. You have to stick holes in it. Much of our work is about taking stereotypes, givens, and problematizing them – mobilizing them is perhaps a better word.

CM: We've recently become aware of audiences who know about our work but have never actually seen a Brith Gof performance. Many more people in Wales have seen our work on television than 'live'. The relationship between this 'distant' audience is complex and is currently intriguing us.

How do you find your audiences in a country that doesn't have a long history of theatre tradition?
CM: We set up alliances in a discursive, collaborative process. *Tri Bywyd* is located in a ruined house on Forestry Commission land – a controversial authority in Wales – so the site is already charged with meaning. We're working with archaeologists from the University of Wales near by, with a dance project and with a local theatre that is also an educational establishment: all these give us inroads to sections of communities that we want to interface with.

The idea of the performance as a final object, the 'be all and end all', just doesn't work with our projects; there are a whole host of other spin-offs. We've been thinking about doing work on radio, CD, television. What does this mean? Are all these peripheral to some kind of holy activity called theatre? Or is theatre there as a 'photo opportunity' for everything else? We move between them all. We often talk about our work as a kind of 'ecology'. I haven't the faintest idea how we'd ever do this sort of work in England: all we do when we go to England is sell a piece of work that we've already made. The most developed manifestations of our work abroad have been in Glasgow: there are similar resonances there to Wales.

Which thinkers and art practices have influenced your work?
CM: We've been influenced by cultural theorists. We looked to them because we work bilingually and we wanted to explore the relationship between the artwork and the constituency. Foucault and Bakhtin have been particularly helpful in terms of working out what it is we are actually doing.

The architect Bernard Tschumi talks about architecture as a hybrid of what is built and what happens there, which is very close to the connections we explore at site. There is the 'host' building and the 'ghost' event we put there. Tschumi's thinking has had a significant impact on our work.

I find it very hard to think of theatre groups who've influenced us. In my case I think the Wooster Group work with an intelligence, setting up fractured fields of activity. They cut and paste, look at things from different angles, and I find that inspiring and exciting.

I have a constant interest in other media, especially film and television. I'm endlessly trying to find the equivalent of an 'edit' in theatre! I try to use film models in our work. What most people like in theatre I actually get frustrated by: they like the fact it's happening in a real space in real time, but I can get quite bored with that.

MP: I came to Cardiff in 1968 to study archaeology. I started making theatre at university, got hold of a copy of Grotowski's *Towards a Poor Theatre* and the rest is history! In that period I found Grotowski's work deeply inspiring. We sat in a darkened room and spent hours trying to work out what he meant and trying out the exercises. At the same time I was aware of the Americans: the Living Theatre, Schechner's Performance Group. My first work was about marrying the two traditions. I suppose at the back of it all is: if all else fails I'll do it myself with a bucket! From the mid-1980s onwards I've been less animated by what calls itself 'theatre' and have become interested in other things. The people I look to are in music. At the moment I'm fascinated by the free jazz musicians. I've been working in a duo with Peter Brötzmann, the German saxophonist. I'm intrigued by the fluidity that free jazz musicians achieve, and am trying to find the equivalent in terms of physical improvisation. I believe in the notion that most art forms tend towards the condition of music.

How has your directing developed over the years?
MP: Our working circumstances have altered constantly, as have the people we've worked with. There wasn't a circuit of playhouses in which I could have developed my craft over thirty years. It's an endless learning process.

CM: There's no theatrical career structure in Wales: we're very close to the street in everything we do.

MP: Allied to that, we are the first generation to bring an experimental theatre practice to maturity. We had no aspirations to jump tracks; we were never preparing ourselves to enter the mainstream. That's one reason we're such a problem for funding bodies.

CM: I think we're proud of the sophistication of our methodology. The funding world tends to be simple-minded. I'm always dismayed by the way they don't understand or engage with our practice. That's one reason that we've been thinking more about publishing materials; just to try and get our ideas across in other ways. The 'opinion-formers' in Wales are not seeing the maturity or breadth of practice in our work. They look at us in banal ways.

MP: But the kind of work we do cannot be represented by a single thing like a script. If you look at the ephemera left behind after a performance we've done, it's in the bodies of performers, in audiences.

The documentation of your work leads you on to another set of problems, doesn't it?
CM: Yes, but it might be valuable that one's practice is again represented by a composite. I think we do our best to make sure that our work is represented in a number of formats.

Do you feel that you can work as you want to in Wales?
CM: Yes and no. We don't have enough money for a permanent ensemble of performers. Five or six permanent performers would be wonderful. We don't have money to do the large-scale, high-profile work which our audience loves. We go through contortions with fund-raising, sponsorship and deals with television companies in order to make work. On the other side of the coin, I am ceaselessly animated and excited by the

cultural context of Wales, stimulated and fed by it. This is an optimistic country with limitless possibilities; there's little cynicism here.

MP: In one sense, we're deeply privileged that we've been able to develop a practice which is fairly unique, but we have also been nimble-footed about the work we do and where.

Do you have obsessions in your work?
MP: I'm very animated by archaeology and the convergencies between archaeology and performance. At a time when 'performance studies' is thrashing around for theories and terminologies, archaeology provides me with useful models.

Recently I've been consumed by some of Dick Hebdige's ideas. He argues that we now live in a society where the only place we can feel safe is 'at home'. He suggests that 'rave culture' is a rush to the communal; that actually it's about being immersed in the mass. I'm wondering whether theatre can reconstitute itself as a 'special world' where partici-pants, so-called, and spectators, so-called, can begin to create manifes-tations of society which are extra-daily; which are not a mirror of life, or indeed anything. Could it be a place where identities are effectively problematized?

You're both very conversant with cultural theory. Why?
CM: Think about film: there's been a detailed, highly intellectual debate in journals such as *Screen* for years, and every aspect of practice is chal-lenged in a wonderful way. I don't see that happening in theatre. In architecture as well there are debates about what the subject is, about how it might be defined. We try to bring a mass of questions to our own work, and we work intelligently, dealing with issues of intertextuality and inter-architecturality. The theories which currently operate at the centre of theatre are not workable for us.

There's a poverty of vocabulary for articulating theatre processes too. I note the way you have invented your own terms.
CM: Yes. We're always thinking about that. We have a kind of shorthand. As I said before, this notion of the well-rounded object in theatre seems dead to us. We're thinking of forms that are discursive, spread out, shows that might last for six hours, and this requires a new language.

How do you see your work developing?
MP: It's a question of recasting the basic contracts: ideas, site, time-length, use of space, audience and performers.

CM: What we're interested in is the theatre *field*, not the object. How can we have a whole array of elements and not one discrete thing? That's what we'll be exploring over the next years.

JONATHAN MILLER

Jonathan Miller was born in London in 1934 and read Natural Sciences at Cambridge University. He qualified as a Doctor of Medicine in 1959. His career has covered many different fields, as author; lecturer and researcher; television producer and presenter; and as director of theatre, opera and film. His reputation as a theatre director was built on his many Shakespeare productions; his *Merchant of Venice* (1970) with Sir Laurence Olivier and Joan Plowright was particularly renowned. From 1988 to 1990 he was Artistic Director of the Old Vic where he directed a number of highly acclaimed productions, including *Andromache* (1988), *The Tempest* (1988), *King Lear* (1989) and Corneille's *The Liar* (1989). In 1973 Miller made his operatic début as a director with Alexander Goehr's *Arden Must Die*. Since then he has directed at many of the world's greatest opera houses; he has established a close relationship with the Maggio Musicale in Florence where he has had successes with *Tosca* (1986), *Don Giovanni* (1990), *Così fan tutte* (1991) and *The Marriage of Figaro* (1992).

What in your view is the task of a director?
Directing is not so much a task as an interest, and theatre for me is about the imagining of possible worlds. A text, a score or a narrative of some sort engages my interest, and my imagination is fired into picturing ways of realizing it in concrete performance. I regard the text as an orphan object which has fallen into my hands and wonder what it means and how it can be brought to life. Sometimes my ideas about realizing a text are influenced by the notion that previous incarnations have not reached its core, or have missed certain areas that I want to explore, so there might be a desire to repudiate the past. I see a text as a promissory note: it exists in some form as a work of art because it left its maker's hand 'finished', but it also points forward to something that has yet to be made, and it is the performance itself that completes the work.

Once you have the text how do you start on the work of realizing its performance?
Work begins in the imagination. The text suggests settings and tones of voice; these loom up and take possession of the mind, and I begin to hear the words spoken in the mouths of imagined people. Once actors are cast, those sounds and images begin to take on more detail than I

could possibly have imagined. I do not work according to a set of principles in the rehearsal room. I used to give long talks about my ideas on
the text, but as I have got older and, I hope, wiser I have become less and
less discursive. Creatively things might feel hesitant and blurred to me,
but I don't want to foreclose the possibility of unforeseen elements
emerging during the course of the rehearsals.

I see the rehearsal room as a playroom; it's rather like a nursery
where I am the supervisor. I let things emerge within a framework.
During rehearsals I might fill the room with books, pictures and repro-
ductions of paintings. At the start I show the actors a model of the set,
the costume designs and perhaps talk about why I might have changed
the historical setting. All this is an introduction to the non-literal meanings in the text. I have found that the more you open yourself up to the
unforeseeable, the more spontaneous and interesting the performance
becomes. Actors cannot be treated as marionettes and I positively want
to encourage the unpredictable eruptions of inspiration that can come
at the most unexpected moments, purely because a group of different
people is working together under pressure.

The process of making a performance is like the growth of a coral
reef; it is not altogether designed. I do not have explicit access to my
own unconscious, but only when I allow for the sudden eruptions from
the unconscious do the organic possibilities for the performance open
themselves up. I think of this in terms of biological evolution, which is
not designed with a foregone conclusion in mind and which gropes its
way to something that only looks inevitable once the journey has been
concluded. I think that rigid directors do a disservice to the process of
creativity and they mistakenly imagine that they have brought everything to the performance. Directors who imagine that their work only
consists in the physical fleshing out of a text are, in my opinion, shutting
down vast areas of creative potential.

Do you research your chosen plays or operas?
I see the whole of my life as being engaged in research. I do not do
'homework' on a specific play. I decide to do a particular play because
over the years I have developed complicated, elaborate ideas on what it
is about. My life is devoted to reading and looking at pictures and from
time to time this culminates in my direction of a play.

At what point does the design concept begin to come into your work?
Usually I have been collaborating with a designer six months before

rehearsals begin. I know the pictures that I want to try to create and I know that I want a particular sort of space; for example, I might know that I want a performance space which is narrow and shallow; or I might be thinking of a space which is deep and unreadable, something like a mannerist painting.

How do you see your role when working with actors?
I suppose I introduce them to things that they don't know. I bring all kinds of different information to them: philosophical, social, political ideas; relations between social classes; historical perspectives. In some ways I am a teacher. Many of my ideas about acting and human behaviour have come from my own very careful observation of others. In many instances I am reminding actors of things that they knew but had forgotten, and in other instances I am asking them to forget what they have learned beforehand if it is obstructing a way forward. Making a performance is a haphazard business. By this I do not mean that chaos reigns, but I do have to be confident that my unconscious is stocked with ideas which will be animated by the pressure and stimulus of working with people in a rehearsal room. My best ideas on productions are never ones for which I have sat down and consciously asked myself: how shall I do this scene? Often a few seconds into the scene material surfaces from some part of me and I suddenly know what needs to be done – it's like the discovery of buried treasure.

Visual arts, in particularly paintings, seem to be a key element in your work as a director.
Paintings have always been important to me. I do not reproduce paintings on stage, but if I'm doing a historical work I draw inspiration from painters and writers working in that period. What I'm seeking is a deep structure which those paintings are expressions of. I might, for example, want to examine what was considered to be an elegant way of standing in the sixteenth and seventeenth centuries. Through studying paintings I would discover that many figures are painted with their hand on their hip, the back of the wrist resting on the hip and the palm of the hand turned outwards. I would find that the courtiers to the king in a painting by Van Dyck stand differently to figures in a painting by Giotto. I would find that the way in which figures are depicted standing varies from culture to culture and can have much to do with politics and class. Paintings are a useful means of learning about the composition of groups of people, about patterns and symmetries.

How aware are you of your audience when you make work?
I think of myself as ordinary and place my trust in my imagination. If an idea appeals to me and my actors become excited about it I take this as the guide that it will connect with the imagination of the audience. I have faith in the audience's ability to recognize ideas that have been hatched in my imagination. I remember when I did a production of *Measure for Measure* (1976) I was pondering over the scene where Claudio, a condemned man, is visited in prison by his sister. I kept asking myself what people do in the terror of expectation. It came to me in a flash: they yawn. This seems to be the opposite reflex of what we might expect, but I thought of how I had felt waiting for an exam to begin, of how others behaved in this tense situation, and I realized that yawning is a nervous action. I saw that for this scene Claudio must sit with his hands between his knees restraining a shuddering yawn. The scene worked and the audience understood what was happening.

Are you aware of influences in your work?
I'm not influenced by other work in the theatre and I do not go and see a great deal. I've learned about directing through watching people. As a doctor I was trained to pick up on minute nuances of human behaviour; I was trained to observe the negligible because precisely that detail may tell an entire story.

If there is a specific named influence in my life then it is the American sociologist Erving Goffman. He has examined the minute details of interpersonal contact and has theorized the ever-present possibility of what he calls 'virtual offence'. This theory looks at the ways in which humans cope with the constant risk of 'offending' others and the way they 'apologize' to others. Goffman argues that we each have a vast barrage of subliminal behaviour to deal with our embarrassment, and he analyses many kinds of interaction and conversation, looking at the ways we defer to each other. I would say that Goffman has been the single strongest influence in the whole of my theatrical life.

When I am working on historical texts there are particular historians I would turn to, such as Braudel, Elias, Lawrence Stone and Kantorowicz's work on kingship and the two bodies of the monarch.

There has been talk of a universality of gesture and body language. What do you think of this?
I think this is naïve primitivism. About 90 per cent of our exchanges are through spoken language; of course the background to that is a physical,

LIVERPOOL JOHN MOORES UNIVERSITY
LEARNING SERVICES

bodily expression, but the cutting edge is the spoken word.

How would you like to develop as a director?
I go from one play to the next. I don't work very much in Britain. I think I'm probably regarded as 'old hat', and journalists here are intensely interested in the 'new thing'. Abroad the attitude to older directors is different and they are cherished for their insights and learning. British theatre is housing a prevailing fashion for an enigmatic and bizarre deconstruction, an impenetrable oddness for its own sake, a kind of neo-neo-neo-Dada! For me the most interesting thing about drama is its intelligibility. When I leave a theatre performance I want to be able to say that I have seen more clearly what it means to be human, what it is like to be us.

KATIE MITCHELL

Born in Reading in 1964, Katie Mitchell studied English Language and Literature at the University of Oxford. She worked as an assistant director to Pip Broughton, Paines Plough and the Royal Shakespeare Company. In 1989 and 1990 she researched director training and rehearsal techniques in Russia, Georgia, Poland and Lithuania. In 1990 she founded Classics on a Shoestring to produce lesser known classics on the London fringe. Her most recent productions include: Henrik Ibsen's *Ghosts* (The Other Place, Royal Shakespeare Company, 1993), John Arden's *Live Like Pigs* (The Theatre Upstairs, Royal Court, 1993), Githa Sowerby's *Rutherford and Son* (Royal National Theatre, 1994), *3 Henry VI* (The Other Place, Royal Shakespeare Company, 1994), August Strindberg's *Easter* (The Pit, 1995), Ernst Toller's *The Machine Wreckers* (Royal National Theatre, 1995), Euripides' *The Phoenician Women* (The Other Place, Royal Shakespeare Company, 1995), Samuel Beckett's *Endgame* (Donmar Warehouse, 1996), *The Mysteries* (The Other Place, Royal Shakespeare Company, 1997) and *Uncle Vanya* (Young Vic, 1998). Her productions of Maxim Gorky's *Vassa Zheleznova* (Gate Theatre, 1990) and Euripides' *Women of Troy* (Gate Theatre, 1991) won a Time Out Award.

What is your principal medium?
Text is my principal medium, but my primary influences are from the field of dance and the avant-garde or physical text work such as that of the Polish director Tadeusz Kantor. Film and mime were also very influential. These are the art forms that drew me into theatre. It was only by chance that I ended up specializing in text.

How do you begin to work on text?
I spend a lot of time researching the background of the text, looking at its historical, socio-political and cultural context. I also look at the autobiographical details of the author's life. I then do a very thorough analysis of the text. If, for example, I am working on a very old text, I look at the etymological root of every single word in it.

What kind of texts have you worked on?
Only once have I done a devised piece, a show about rape, *Gobstopper*

(1986), written by Juliet Towhidi. Apart from that I've only worked on texts written before the 1950s. This is chance, not choice, as I read as many contemporary plays as I do classical. The reasons I choose to do one text rather than another are very subjective, but there is normally a connection between the subject matter and what is going on outside in the community.

What interests you about starting from text rather than from something else?
Text is freedom within form. If I wasn't involved in theatre I would be an archaeologist or an anthropologist. I love the idea of starting with a text that I know very shallowly and spending hours and hours digging deeper and deeper into it, opening lots of doors into its possible meanings. I love that process intellectually and emotionally. I love the preparation and I love the work with the actors.

I go on a journey with each text I work on. To take Ibsen's *Ghosts* (1993) as an example, the first thing I did was to get someone to do a literal translation to bring it as close to Norwegian as possible. Then I found someone to read it to me in Norwegian in order to give me a sensual impression of the language to complement my intellectual understanding of it. I also did a great deal of research into that period of history that bred the heart and mind of Ibsen. I made field trips to Norway, looked at the art of the period, recorded birds and took photographs of the place, Rosendal, where it is thought the play might have been set. I studied the light, recorded measurements of the temperature and looked at the landscape, flowers, plants, animals. I try to get as close to the text as I can from as many different angles as possible.

What is theatre for you?
Stories, first and foremost. The stories may or may not be text-based. You can also have visual stories, musical stories or multi-media stories, and the stories don't have to be literal, with a series of logically connected events, but can also be metaphorical or poetic. As a director my job is to find the best form in which to tell the story that I have chosen. Theatre is the telling of stories by one section of the community to another.

What are the guiding principles of your directing practice?
I always work collaboratively with a team of people including a set designer, a lighting designer, a sound designer, a musical director and a movement director. In the field trips, for instance, I try to travel with as many members of this team as possible so that we can all absorb as many

of the potential meanings of the text as possible. I believe collaboration to be at the heart of my work both outside and inside the rehearsal room. The working environment has to be egalitarian: everybody has to have equal input into the work. In the end it is very difficult to define who is doing what: who is directing, who is leading the movement, who is leading the music – there is a lot of cross-over. This is the key principle of my practice.

On the other hand, this is a very transitional moment for me. I find myself less and less interested in working in established theatre environments. There is something about the ritual of going to the theatre, buying a ticket and so on that is quite alienating for large sections of the community. I am beginning to doubt whether the theatre structures as they stand are the best places in which to make theatre; they are based on old-fashioned structures and rituals, and I think we need something new in terms of form and content trying to break them.

How do you work with the actors?
The basis is equality in the rehearsal room. In the first two weeks of rehearsal nobody touches their own character. This is something many directors do to avoid a hierarchical situation on the basis of the number of lines actors have to say. I am interested in the group engaging in the whole play and not just in their individual characters. Only later do the actors work on how their characters function within the play. I tend to be more interested in actors who are committed to the play first, and to their characters second. I am interested in them being as obsessional as possible about all the different routes that lead to the making of a play.

If I were to classify my technique, I would say that it is based on the Stanislavski system. In life we usually use language in order to effect a change in the person or persons we are talking to. Most of what we say has a visible or invisible intention: sometimes we say what we mean and at other times we say one thing and mean something completely different. Amongst other things, Stanislavski analysed our use of language in life and created an acting system based on his analysis. He separated out the text (what we say) from the subtext (what we intend by what we say) and he called our intentions 'objectives'. Every line an actor says on stage has an objective behind it. It is this system that I use in rehearsals, because for me it is the exchange of something living between characters on stage that produces the most interesting theatre.

Do you think there is such thing as a universal performance language?
I have no idea because I have never explored this issue. I was fascinated by Peter Brook's *Conference of the Birds* which searched for a universal performance language, but I feel that in order to answer that question one would probably have to undergo a series of practical baptisms. I mean that one would have to take what one might think approaches a universal performance language around the universe. I am not sure that there is a possible answer to be given unless one undergoes that practical experience.

Has your notion of directing changed over the years?
I came to directing when I was about fifteen years old and this was because I really wanted to be a painter, but I couldn't draw. One day I took a stage play and painted a picture with it. That's when it all started. It was pure chance! By the time I directed my first professional piece, I had become much more pro-actor than pro-image. Now I am going through a period of transition, but I don't know where it's going to lead.

When I first did work on the fringe I was more rigorous, but working under immense pressure in big organizations has somehow softened some of that rigour, sometimes to the detriment of the work. I am not suggesting that one should be tyrannical, but I do believe that one has to be very rigorous and not worry whether one is or isn't liked by the actors. When you have success early in your career, you are catapulted into situations where you are working with incredibly experienced and skilled actors and you are not always ready for that. You can back off slightly and your confidence can drop because you feel that you should be in a position of humility. That's right on one level, but it has consequences in the way one works.

How does awareness of audience affect your work?
I watch the audience like a hawk, trying to determine who they are. My primary responsibility is towards them: it is a responsibility of clarity, precision and narrative.

To explain this I'll describe something that happened while I was directing *Rutherford and Son* (1994). This is a searing left-wing anti-capitalist play which pivots around a man who runs a glass factory. He abuses his workers and he abuses his family, particularly the women. He is an incredibly sexist man. The woman who wrote it, Githa Sowerby, didn't want the capitalist man to be too mono-dimensional, so she fleshed out the character and gave him sympathetic scenes, trying to help the audience to understand why this man was behaving the way he was. When the play first opened, the balance was very accurate, for example it was very clear that the production wasn't in any way wishing to condone his behaviour. But because of the social background and the make-up of the audience who come to the Royal National Theatre, bit by bit the meaning of the piece changed and in the end became a celebration of that man as opposed to a condemnation of him. I hadn't seen the piece for about a month, which is very unusual for me, and when I came back there was something deeply wrong in the way in which the dialogue was flowing. What had happened was that the audience was willing the performers to change the bias of the play.

I remember vividly one woman who was in a red suit with a golden butterfly jumping up and down on her chest every time she moved: she was looking at my jeans in absolute disgust because she had to sit next to me. Observing her and her husband watching the piece I realized that whenever this man, Rutherford, inflicted something brutal on the other characters the man and the woman were nodding, smiling and agreeing with him. I talked to the actors at length. It wasn't their fault, but the space in between them and the audience had changed. The audience had willed them in a direction in which they didn't want to go. Bob Peck, who was playing the part of Rutherford, took the problem very seriously and decided to stop dwelling on certain lines, thus bringing the emphasis back to where it had been. It's a bit like working with a very sophisticated computer: you are continually adjusting a huge amount of buttons in order to prevent something like this from occurring. It took us a while, but I think we finally succeeded.

The most exciting thing for me on a stage is the space in between the characters; this is why I am interested in objectives. They make characters very dynamic, actively trying to transform, provoke or infect other characters. For me it's what occurs in between two or more people that is exciting. The nature of the space between the actors and the audience is the same. When there is a vacuum between what is happening on stage and the audience there is something fundamentally wrong with the medium.

Who and what have acted as influences on your work?
Even on my way to this interview I was researching Beckett's *Endgame*. I saw this fantastic old man dressed in black who looked as if he had just

walked out of *Waiting for Godot*. Then I saw this other old man, bare-foot, carrying two pink blankets. A few days ago a bomb exploded in the Isle of Dogs. Everything I experience as a member of a community has a direct influence on the work I do.

Naturally, I am also influenced by other practitioners: Deborah Warner, Steven Daldry, Pete Brooks and, on the continent, Pina Bausch, Peter Brook, Peter Stein, Ariane Mnouchkine, Tadeusz Kantor and Anatoly Vasilyev.

There is something about repetition, repeated gestures in Bausch's work that I find fascinating, as well as the collision between big events and very simple activities, like standing and peeling an onion. In Mnouchkine's work I like the environment that she creates around her theatre and the fact that the actors also build the set, and make the props and the costumes. I love the way she welcomes the audience into her building. I love the food, the décor, the music, the pre-play experience and the way it prepares the audience to receive her work. In Brook I love the fact that he is very pure and incredibly simple: pure in the sense that he has a lucidity of thought. Peter Stein I love for the absolute thoroughness in the preparation of his work on Chekhov. It's phenomenal: when he did Chekhov he took the entire ensemble to Yalta to absorb Russian culture.

One of the great joys of my time in Eastern Europe was to have the possibility of spending two weeks watching Vasilyev work. It seems to me that he works by immersion, which I find an interesting process. When I was there, every single morning they sang Russian orthodox harmonies. His process resembles the way salt or dust settles in water. It requires an incredible amount of preparation and reading. Vasilyev also engages in his work on a metaphysical level which I find extraordinary.

The most important formative experience I had was when I was doing my training as an assistant director and I got a grant to go to Eastern Europe – Poland, Georgia, Lithuania and Russia. It was 1989, a very important time for those countries. I went to this small Polish village called Gardzienice, near Lublin, in the south-east of Poland. I spent a considerable time there with a company also called Gardzienice, watching them do practical, physical exercises. They had developed the legacy of Grotowski; their work was a collision between para-theatrical work and physical training and drew on the music and stories of dying ethnic minority communities all over the world. That had a phenomenal impact on me.

What is your interest in languages?

After my experience with Gardzienice, Paul Allain, who was studing Gardzienice for his PhD, and I took a half-Polish, half-English company around villages in Poland. We decided to base our story around three Polish words: God, apple and bread. Then we took a simple myth, 'Diarmuid and Graine', an Irish version of Tristan and Isolde, and tried to tell its story using those three words, movement, dance and singing. Most of the work was movement-based and not text-based, so language wasn't such a great barrier.

How do you see yourself in terms of the European theatrical/performance landscape?

It is difficult to respond to this question, because as a director you don't spend much time 'seeing yourself'. When I did *Henry VI*, part 3 (1994), it was received in a very confused way in Britain. On the continent it was received much more positively. I spent hours trying to work out why and I don't think I have an accurate answer, but I believe that it's probably because there is a literalness in audiences in the United Kingdom that you don't get on the continent.

Do you feel you can work as you want to work in this country?

This is a two-level question. One level is about economics and asks whether I can afford to work in this country; the other is about art. I am in a very exclusive situation because I can get paid for what I do. Aesthetically, perhaps there are problems. If you don't want to do things that are part of the prevailing patterns, values or tastes then it's not always easy. There are invisible taste structures and values, and you don't know that you are running up against them until it happens. So the answer to the second part of the question depends on how brave I am. It's great being in the situation where there is no problem about getting a job, but sometimes I think I really want to do a piece of work in a warehouse and I bottle out because it's easier to do it as a paid piece of work in a theatre.

What would you hope to see developing in terms of the director in the future?

I would welcome training courses based on the Russian system. In Russia directors receive a five-year training, starting with a year of basic acting classes followed by a programme of work which includes textual analysis, research/preparation, lighting, set design, stage craft and the history of world theatre. This gives aspiring directors a very strong basis from which to start practising their craft professionally.

What do you like about the Stanislavskian approach?
Stanislavski looked at acting and directing as a science. There is no mystery in a lot of what he says. He spent several years analysing the craft and the results are very useful. Of course this isn't the only way of working, but his approach does offer a very solid foundation for rehearsals. If his techniques start to restrict actors they should be discarded. I think its advantage is that it gives an initial shared language to the actors and the directors and provides a place to start from. Then, as rehearsals continue, you can develop a more individualized system or method of work.

What are your preoccupations as a director?
As a director I think that I have to keep working on myself as a human being, to improve my capacities to direct, to get better at the craft. This can preoccupy you for a whole lifetime.

I have been very preoccupied with family structures. For me these represent a microcosm of social structures that fascinate me. Politically, I am fascinated by the issue of what is going to replace Russian and East European communism. I am very frightened by nationalism and the spate of civil wars globally. I vowed that as long as the war in the former Yugoslavia was continuing I would do an anti-civil war, or anti-war play every year. So families, the Left, nationalism and war are my four major preoccupations.

GERRY MULGREW

Born in 1951 in Glasgow, Gerry Mulgrew read French and Philosophy
at Glasgow University, followed by studies at the Sorbonne. Between
1975 and 1980 he worked with Theatre Workshop in Edinburgh;
between 1980 and 1982 he was with Pocket Theatre, Cumbria; and
from 1982 to 1983 he was with Welfare State International, working,
amongst other things, as a metaphysical bingo caller and a ritual fire
sculpture animateur. In 1983 he co-founded Communicado, and was
Artistic Director until 1998. The company created over twenty-one
productions and won many awards, including six Fringe Firsts. His
work in the theatre has been hugely diverse; he has worked as a director, writer, musician, deviser and actor in community theatre, mainstream theatre and opera. His work as a freelance director includes
Moby Dick (1993–4) for the Royal Shakespeare Company.

Is there a primary medium in your directing?
I suppose I gravitate between text and non-text! I've constantly tried to
experiment, which means sometimes I've started with text and at other
times I've worked from an idea, or I've used devising as a way into
something.

To give you some examples, I did a two-man show *A Wee Home from
Home* (1989), and worked with a dancer and a singer-songwriter. We
wrote the songs as we went along. Then, a few years ago, there was *The
Legend of St Julian* (1993), a piece I based on a short story by Flaubert,
which I tried to interpret with hardly any language. We devised a movement style, and combined live music with a dense recorded tape – we
had continuous sound for one and a half hours. I didn't prepare a script,
but I experimented with different parts of the story, and examined non-
verbal ways of telling it. In the end the story was interpreted through
movement, sound, light, colour and moving scenery. It was like a
strange hallucinogenic experience! I found the psychology of light fascinating: the effect of performers moving in and out of the light, of movement out of darkness. My imagination has always wanted a huge
landscape to work with, somewhere that allowed for rapid moves
between different times, places and realities.

Is narrative important to you?
Yes and no. In all these elements of text, physicality, dance and music I'm trying to find connections and common threads, searching for the unfindable. Whether I work with or without text I'm seeking an anchor in the heart of a story. But I'm also interested in reaching beyond narrative, if you like. I did a piece called *Jock Tamson's Bairns* for the Glasgow City of Culture festivities in 1990. It was an attempt to work a narrative in a different way, using memories, ghosts, illusions. It was really a staged poem about Scotland; a crazy landscape which attempted to convey the psychological picture of a nation. I centred it round a Burns supper and set it in Hell. That was my biggest leap into the dark as a director; it was a very visceral piece with a cast of twenty-five.

What is theatre for you?
Sometimes I think it has replaced Catholicism in my life, particularly when I review my use of sacrificial and redemptive imagery. I'm drawn to a theatre of death and rebirth.

I started out as an actor in children's theatre – and many would say I never left it! I learned *in situ*, in a wonderful, playful world of invention: you could use any style, do anything as long as it worked. I developed a specific idea about text during that time: theatre can't just be spoken, children get bored of that very quickly. So I worked on physical expression, music, magic and the imagination. Theatre, at its best, is a gateway into a different world of the imagination – and that world can be used in different ways. I think audiences yearn for another world, and in a sense that isn't necessarily escapist. I found I could use the created world to demonstrate something, and I believe that expressing a morality is a function of theatre. There has to be a purpose behind a piece, it's not just a magic show: if purpose and imagination come together well, then theatre can be a very powerful medium. There's a Scottish word, *ceilidh*; a *ceilidh* can be a meeting place where stories and ideas are shared. That might seem sentimental, but in my vision theatre is a place where people come to meet themselves or to see themselves. Each theatre has a place in its own community.

What does it mean to be a director?
It means I make the final decisions about things. I decide on the meaning of a piece. It's to do with a collaboration between the director's 'eye' outside and the living bodies of the performers on the inside. I work very much as a collaborator with other actors, whether I'm in the per-

formance or not. I love performing, and being a director has grown from that. I started directing because I felt it was the only way I could express myself fully. I had that insight which perceives certain ways of interaction and the rhythms. I think directing is very akin to musical composition; mixing all these elements of text, sound, light and movement is very complex and you need to be able to find rhythms to knit them together. Those rhythms are redefined with each generation.

Directing is multi-layered, it's a continual search for a mechanism to unlock what's underneath the surface of a play or an idea. I remember when I directed Liz Lochhead's *Mary Queen of Scots Got her Head Chopped off* (1987), it was the first time I had a dancer in the cast. It was very difficult to get a sense of common rhythm between the dancer and the actors: the dancer couldn't get over the amount of discussion between the actors; he communicated by moving his body but the actors wanted to talk and talk. As a director you have to be searching constantly for modes of language that are more fluid than the purely verbal. There is a lot of collaboration in my work, but in order for a powerful creation to come about, a made object, there has to be a stamp on it. I don't know that it's ever possible to be a democrat as a director. It's hard, you make decisions, but audiences react more truthfully to something which is strong.

How important is audience to you?
That's why I do theatre. My awareness of the audience goes in ebbs and flows. Ultimately, you have to show something and it has to work. Sometimes I do things to please the audience, at other times I explore things for myself, things which reflect my own sense of truth. Who knows what that audience is? Is it the mass or just one particular person?

Where does working in Scotland fit into all this?
Since it was set up, Communicado's work has been a constant: an endeavour to create one part of a new Scottish repertoire. It's a break away from the dominance of English theatre traditions and their models in every sense – speech, behaviour and subject matter in particular. First and foremost I wanted to speak to Scottish people, but I soon saw that you have to go beyond this. My involvement has been political, but I've also always seen it to be a huge advantage that Scottish theatre has no looming shadows, no Shakespeare. We could invent anything we liked! Being a director is like fumbling around in the dark with no torch but a

strong grip once you've found something – that's the best way to describe it.

I suppose I've been looking for a new poetic form. Certainly with *Mary Queen of Scots Got her Head Chopped off*, I worked very closely on structure with the writer and I was thinking in terms of a ballad play; I was looking for ideas on how to work Scottish rhythms of speech and song into a more fluid theatrical form. This may sound as though I'm floating off in the clouds, but I also like my theatre to be what I call 'on the ground'. Some time ago I acted in a Communicado production of Athol Fugard's play *A Place with the Pigs* (1994–5). It's a two-hander with a strong allegorical aspect, and could be called poetic. It included a brass band. I like that mix of the extraordinary, the poetic and the strong narrative. Shakespeare was capable of breathtaking flights of thought, but his characters are made of flesh and blood.

Who has influenced your work?
You could say that John McGrath's 7:84 theatre company was the first influence on me. I remember seeing *The Cheviot, the Stag, and the Black, Black Oil*. I'd never seen theatre like that in my life: spoken in our own Scottish voices and so full of music! It didn't seem like a play. Here was this explosion of joy, anger, politics, humour, everything, and with a *ceilidh* afterwards – it was quite extraordinary, a different kind of theatrical event. It was the anger boiling beneath it that was the most invigorating aspect. Now that kind of theatre has been superseded by something else, and today's directors are searching for different modes of expression and new forms.

Besides this, many in this book have influenced me. The most devastating influence, however, was Tadeusz Kantor's *Dead Class*.

Are there themes that you come back to again and again in your work?
Sex and death, basically. Oh, and food! What else is there? I like theatre which goes to the edge, which goes to the limits of human endurance for both actors and audience. Humour can also be vital; if someone in the audience is literally helpless with laughter the whole experience is opened up for them. Laughter is a showman's instinct, of course. I'd actually like to push and explore a darker side in my work. It's a question of balancing rhythms between light and dark, subtle and vulgar, fast and slow. It's very hard trying to describe what you do as a director. My theatre is like the *Rite of Spring* with bits of vaudeville thrown into it.

I suppose I'm obsessed with getting things a thousand times better. I want to see theatre respond to the challenges thrown at it by film and television. We have to find revolutionary new forms in order to take up that challenge. Theatre must become irresistible to us.

Where do you see yourself in terms of a wider theatrical landscape?
As a director you can't do anything else but start in the skin you were born with, which for me is Scots. Knowing who you are and where you're from is critical. But you also have to be in dialogue; it's about looking in and looking out. What I do is part of the mosaic of British and then European theatre, which has a particular emphasis and quality to it.

Can you work as you want to in Britain?
No. One reason is funding and the other, the main reason, is the result of a particular attitude. Theatre is not regarded as important enough by the people of Britain. It's to do with a lack of resources, serious thinking, the lack of facility to work as an ensemble (which I greatly value), the lack of shared knowledge and learning rather than training. In Scotland I constantly meet actors who are frustrated, who feel that they can't work to their full potential. A good part in a play is rare. There is an extraordinary amount of energy to tap and too much of it goes to waste. All too often I see a mediocre director in charge of talented actors. Someone said to me recently that the director's role is the easiest to hide behind; at the end of the day it's the actors who have to perform. I think this mainstream movement towards director training, which professes to be 'intellectual' and 'textual', needs to be balanced by the physical and the visual. Someone once said that on the day of the first encounter between director and performers, the director should have unlimited faith but absolutely no idea whatsoever of how they're going to do the play or performance piece. Each process is different from the last; you start again and throw assumptions and preconceived ideas out of the window.

There has been fantastic theatre on these islands for centuries, and the British need to have more confidence in that. Maybe the actors need to take hold of the theatre again. People aren't being invested in, and that's what theatre is more than anything else.

LLOYD NEWSON

Lloyd Newson was born in Albury, Australia. His interest in dance
arose while he was completing his degree in psychology at Melbourne
University. This interest led to a scholarship with the London School
of Contemporary Dance and he came to Britain in 1980. From 1981 to
1985 he was a dancer and choreographer with Extemporary Dance
Theatre, and during this time he worked with a wide range of choreographers, including Karole Armitage, Michael Clark, David Gordon,
Daniel Larrieu and Dan Wagoner. Since 1986 his work as the Director of London-based DV8 Physical Theatre has had a dynamic impact
on contemporary dance by challenging the traditional aesthetics and
forms which pervade most modern and classical dance. His stage and
film work with DV8 have consistently won major British and international awards.

What are the concerns in your work?
They have varied over the years. Between 1986 and 1990 I began with
generalized themes rather than scripted scenarios. *My Sex, Our Dance*
(1986) questioned how much you can trust someone. We used the ana-
logy of physical risk-taking – how far you could push your body, somebody, the 'body' before it became dangerous. *My Body, Your Body* (1987)
was inspired by Robin Norwood's book *Women Who Love Too Much*,
which explored the psychology of women who seek relationships with
abusive men. I used tape-recorded interviews with a close woman friend
as the initial stimulus for the work. There wasn't a storyline as such; its
links were more thematic than narrative. For *Dead Dreams of Mono-
chrome Men* (1988) I'd read Brian Masters' book, *Killing for Company*,
about mass-murderer Dennis Nielson. In my mind I saw connections
between this and the debates then taking place in Parliament on Clause
28; those debates revolved round issues of repression, loneliness and
restriction of freedom – to name but a few. After *If Only* (1990), which
was loosely about faith, and the need to believe in someone or something, I felt that I couldn't go back into the studio without a well-
planned, detailed storyline. I didn't want to repeat material, and finding
new things to explore required more investigation, more time and new
working approaches.

For *Strange Fish* (1992) I wrote the scenario in advance and Wendy Houstoun helped in the redrafts. I knew that I wanted a religious figure to reflect both light and darkness, faith and faithlessness. An outline made the process easier. I still used improvisation but was able to divide my ideas more clearly. The improvisations became more structured and precise. Again, for *Enter Achilles* (1995) I wrote a scenario; of course, not everything you write on paper can be successfully translated into movement, but I knew I wanted to explore the duality of men: the repulsive, the dangerous, the frightening mixed with the attractive facets of masculinity. Discoveries need to be incorporated that emerge from rehearsals and it's important not to deny these. I know roughly where I am heading before I begin a project, although a performer's individual contribution may change what events occur within the piece considerably. Usually I'm open to changes, and structures have to be loose enough to accommodate these changes and input from the performers. The creative process must be one of discovery rather than me just blindly forcing my beliefs and preconceptions on others in order to fit a written structure.

What are you committed to during the rehearsal process?
Finding fresh ways of saying things that resonate with the performers' own truths. The performers' creativity and devising as a process are what excite me about the way DV8 work. With a traditional play you have to follow the writer's journey. I've given up saying, 'Move like this', and 'Here are the steps; learn them.' This allows the performers a greater sense of ownership and authenticity over the final material. But what you see every night on stage is set, as any slight change in the movement could throw the story off. There are no dictionaries for physical movement like there are for words, so I struggle to find what I've called 'specific ambiguity' – this can hold the story together and at the same time allow individual audience members to have their own reading of what's happening.

How would you describe your work?
DV8 were one of the first groups in Britain to call their work physical theatre, which is a Grotowski-based term. Now it's a term I'm hesitant to use because of its current overuse and abuse to describe almost anything that isn't dance or traditional theatre. My physical work requires trained dancers, although many trained dancers can't do it because they've lost the connection between meaning and movement. Theatre

and dance forms are still highly regimented, and I'd like to see more cross-form work, but it's hard to find performers who have the range, skills and courage to cross forms. Many dancers and actors are not interested in exploring new ground: they say, 'Give me the steps' and 'Where's the script?' I'm not interested in setting movement or words that other people imitate – they can't be me and I can't be them. Dance often prevents you from seeing the individual, and it's the person that I'm interested in; what their life story is, what's inside their head, not the reduction of people through (limited) form. What fascinates me is *who* the performers are, and the style of the company will vary depending on the amalgamation of those performers. None of us move in the same way: I want to acknowledge the differences and what they mean, not eradicate them. It is this approach, I believe, that allows us to see and understand individuals over form.

What is your main method of working in rehearsal?
Improvisation. I come in with some sort of structure. For example, I might want to work on the physicality of 'greetings'. I extend the improvisations as far as they will go. Perhaps from shaking hands to patting. I explore what happens to the changes in rhythm. What happens if the action remains the same but the speed or quality changes? What are acceptable and unacceptable places to touch when greeting, and why? Meeting, greeting, bonding, fighting, confusion, danger – a simple idea which can lead on to a huge range of possibilities. I try to structure the devising day by finding a balance between the physical, psychological and emotional demands on the performers.

For *Enter Achilles* we did a whole set of improvisations around the pint glass. The pint is very British, but what else does it represent culturally, in itself? It can be both fragile and strong, lethal or beautiful. Likewise with the rope work in *Enter Achilles* there were a whole range of questions I was asking about support. When is it acceptable for men to hold hands in public? In acrobatic work the context allows it – lives are at stake – but the same action on the ground changes the meaning completely. In rehearsals there is constant discussion with the performers to make sure that we all understand what is going on; this is more common in theatre, but uncommon in dance.

There are many physical metaphors embedded in language, and I might use these as a starting-point, for example, 'head over heels in love' or 'at an arm's length'. I might also use experiences that my performers tell me about from their own or others' lives. The attack on the inflatable doll in *Enter Achilles* came straight from an event that a friend of mine experienced.

We have always had a video camera to record our improvisations: hence our name DV8 – dance and video eight. Reviewing a three-hour improvisation may only reveal twenty seconds of useful material, which we then might build on.

How would you differentiate your work from that of other practitioners?
Set design has become more integral to my work. I'm interested in the relationship between architecture and the body, and we've explored many different types of aerial work. My work is extremely imagistic – the set is necessary to place the movement in an environment which helps to create a series of connected visual associations. Jack Thompson's work as lighting designer has been critical in helping us to create atmosphere and highlight meaning. We sometimes use language, though our work is not reliant on text. Since 1987 we've always commissioned scores for our performances and experimented with music and voice, and ways in which these can combine with movement.

The form of contact work we use is not one that most other companies use; DV8's contact work is developmental and I would argue that this is not the norm. I'm not a purist: I don't rely on just one movement style. How we train depends on the subject matter we're exploring at the time; I'm always looking for different ways to see and train the body. In the past we've incorporated yoga into the training and such skills as rope work, Irish dancing and aerobic workouts as well as the usual ballet, contemporary and contact improvisation techniques.

Why did you choose to work in the United Kingdom?
Because of the opportunities that were available to me. The quality and quantity of the artists, set and lighting designers in Europe is extraordinary compared to Australia. The grant DV8 receives from the Arts Council amounts to the entire budget available for independent companies in Australia – which probably accounts for why so much dance talent leaves Australia. We tour non-stop. I wouldn't be able to do that if we were based in Sydney. In the last nine years the company's profile has been high and the opportunities available to us have been phenomenal. The film of *Strange Fish* won the Prix Italia and our work has made the front page of the tabloids, which proves that dance can have an effect in the wider world and act as a political force instead of reflecting the usual abstraction and 'niceness' – which speaks of little to very few.

How have you developed in your work?

On a good day I'd like to think very well! I'm certainly more analytical about movement now, and see the possibilities of exploring movement in many different contexts, which I wouldn't have seen eight years ago. I've been able to refine skills, incorporate humour and speak about broader issues. I look back on *MSM* (1993) and the problems of testimonials and set text, but it was a piece that dealt with important social issues at the time, and it taught me a lot about the relationship between text and movement. I'm wary of words but I don't want to shy away from using them altogether. If they're necessary why not incorporate them? I want to keep moving all the time, keep surprising myself, and working with different people in different ways helps to achieve this.

My background in psychology has provoked me constantly to ask 'why?' Why do people move? Why do people do arabesques? I left traditional dance because of its lack of specificity, its lack of questioning and its lack of rigour beyond technique. My psychology training helps me to analyse relationships between performers quickly, to see patterns of behaviour and language and think of physical ways to interpret these.

What are your thoughts on audience?

With *Enter Achilles* I made a decision to keep the audience entertained, and what that really meant was keeping myself entertained. I used to do very 'enduring' performances, but I need something different now. I need to be able to laugh about hitting my head against a brick wall – distance and balance help us see pain in perspective.

When we presented *MSM* in the West End I was told that we couldn't do anything 'illicit or obscene' – their words, not mine. In case we might offend the audience we had to have a lawyer present in the dress rehearsals advising us on what was 'decent' and what was not. That experience made me determined not to compromise my work in the future, even if it means foregoing large amounts of money for the company, and perhaps results in smaller audiences.

Every dance company or theatre venue presents its politics, whether consciously or not, but DV8's politics are definitely not mainstream. I'm pleased our work has an edge to it – thought-provoking work will upset and create factions. What are the politics of point shoes and tutus in traditional ballet? Every aesthetic has a politics, but most dancers and choreographers do not question the politics/aesthetic they employ and have been trained in. I don't know that I could justify an arabesque in *Enter Achilles*, though all the performers could execute it. Skill-display in dance too often overrides meaning. I fight to present reality as I see it in the world around me, and if it offends people they can stay away or shut their eyes and put their fingers in their ears.

Who has influenced you?
Pina Bausch. She's changed how we perceive theatre and dance. She brings together great technicians who are not obsessed with showing off their techniques. I was also influenced by Anne Teresa De Keersmaeker's early work: there was something extraordinary in how she used repetition. Unfortunately, for many contemporary choreographers the risk element in their work is to do with physical risk as opposed to content. For me it's important that my content is as challenging as the physical aspects of the work. I enjoyed Pete Brooks's work when Impact Theatre Company were together. Tim Etchells has also produced some remarkable performances.

How do you see yourself in relation to other practitioners?
I think we've had a strong influence on dance and on some theatre in England. Acting schools now incorporate physical theatre practitioners into their courses, and the Royal Shakespeare Company have a stronger physical component in their training these days.

I trained in contemporary dance and worked with over twenty-six different choreographers, many of whom were of international standing, but I left mainstream dance because it didn't satisfy me. Why do older performers decide not to stay in dance? I don't think it's only about the deterioration of the body. Too many of those working in dance are concerned with superficial issues – with youth and beauty, with making pretty pictures and shapes. Rarely does dance address the complexities of the real world. At times dance feels very juvenile to me: until we redefine our notions of what a dancer looks like and how a dancer moves; until older dancers can be encouraged to keep performing and to talk about their lives, most forms of Western dance will remain young and immature. We must encourage dancers to use more than just their bodies. We need to break down the hierarchy within dance through intelligent and democratic work.

Can you work as you want to in this country?
Yes. The only problem is finding the calibre of performer and dancer who wants to do more than just copy someone else's steps. I look to other countries more and more, as there aren't many dancers in Britain who can think/move in a manner beyond their original training. It's also

partly this inability to readapt that makes it difficult to find more mature, open-minded dancers.

What are your preoccupations as a director?

If I'm being general and thereby reductive, I'd say that *MSM* considered gender, the body, sexuality and secrets. Other works have dealt with issues of faith and morality, the use and abuse of power, and the oppression of minority groups in society. While my preoccupations might not have changed over the years, my style of presenting them has. It seems that my pieces often raise issues that people would rather avoid. I worked for a year as a therapist but became disillusioned with the classic therapeutic model and its effectiveness. I wanted to work with people in a different and more experimental way. My form of theatre is regularly likened to therapy, and I don't view that as a criticism or a problem. Shouldn't art ultimately be about helping us to understand one another, and preventing us from causing harm to ourselves and others? So at the expense of sounding pretentious I suppose I'm concerned with how theatre can help me/us grow. I hope theatre is more than what David Hare once described it as: a haven for the neurotic and narcotic.

How do you hope to develop?

With a lot of work! If I could anticipate how I'd develop, I'd stop now. My greatest concern is not to repeat myself. I want my language to become more sophisticated; I want to find more physical ways of talking about emotional and psychological states. Obviously this invokes environmental and socio-political issues, given that they have a direct impact on the way people behave. There aren't many people doing this in dance. That's good because it means there's plenty of room to make discoveries.

Julia Pascal

Julia Pascal was born in Manchester in 1949, attended the E15 Acting School in London and read English at London University. She writes for stage, film and radio, and has directed extensively in London and abroad. She was the first woman to direct a piece at the National Theatre with her own dramatized platform performance of Dorothy Parker's *Men Seldom Make Passes* (1978). In 1983 she founded the Pascal Theatre Company and directed her trilogy of Holocaust plays, *Theresa* (1990), *A Dead Woman on Holiday* (1991) and *The Dybbuk* (1992). In 1994 she directed *L'Annee Zero*, followed by an adaptation of *Villette* (1996) and *St Joan* (1997). Currently, she is working on *The Yiddish Queen Lear* (1999).

What is it that drives your directing practice?
More and more I think theatre is about creating atmosphere, whether it's my own plays or others that I'm directing. I have an interest in texts that bite and have a self-mocking humour; in people who are victims but resist through gravelly humour. In *Theresa* (1990), the first part of my Holocaust trilogy, I knew that I wanted to capture the atmosphere of pre-war Britain and Central Europe. When I auditioned Ruth Posner with her thick white hair, her Polish face and accent I knew that she could be a part of the atmosphere that I was after. The look of an actor interests me greatly. I realized some time into the productions about the Holocaust that my perspective of the history is very much through a woman's eyes.

Do you follow certain principles in the rehearsal rooms?
I do try to set up a democratic forum where everyone can contribute, but it's hard to control. I suppose it's semi-benevolent authoritarianism! I never block, I let the actors find their own space relationships. I don't give line readings unless the actor is having a particular problem. I make actors aware of the different rhythms of movement they have from one another and try to make them physically aware of the character they are playing, perhaps in something as simple as the way of walking. I'm fluid and experiment in many ways before making a final decision. I tend to work by instinct rather than analysis.

I always walk into the rehearsal room with an open mind. I'm prepared to change, to listen to new ideas and thoughts. There's no blueprint in my mind that I seek to reproduce.

I'm at my happiest during the technical run and ideally would spend two weeks on the piece at this point! I often make quite radical changes at the technical rehearsal, perhaps writing and/or cutting a scene. I see the work very clearly at the technical rehearsal and in a way that I don't beforehand. I'll be seeking a balance between scenes and spend hours on the details of lighting and sound.

How do you see your role as director?
I don't plan what I'm going to do during rehearsals. I give my actors a lot of space to invent for themselves. I find myself listening very closely to my actors, absorbing the atmosphere that they are giving out. I'm the director as psychiatrist; I filter back what they come up with in a more concentrated form. My work is about unlocking the unconscious in an actor and enabling them to reach for a depth of creativity. If actors hit a problem in the text I often make them tell me their dreams or memories and work on their hidden fears and emotions. I ask them if there are ways in which they can connect their feelings with the text. In Ruth Posner's case I got her to talk about her childhood in the Warsaw ghetto. I made her tell it in Polish. I then wrote half the scene and made the actors improvise the rest.

I direct with a strong sense of rhythm and sound; I can hear the musicality of a piece of work. I know if a word is missing or if one of the actors is speaking out of key. My feeling for image is also extremely important and my actors often tell me that I give very strange instructions, such as: 'Be a window', or 'Be the voice of ancient Egypt', or 'Put on the mask of WOMAN!' In *Theresa* there is a scene where a Nazi soldier seduces a young Guernsey girl; the actor was being far too nice. In the end I told him, 'You're forty and you don't smile' – he understood instantly. Actors tell me that I trust them and that this allows them to give. They also tell me that I work by instinct and intuition, trying to give a sense of what is behind the words as opposed to an emphasis on hollow delivery. I don't bully but I do insist – gently!

I direct with a strong sense of the whole but have an acute eye for detail, especially in terms of how an actor moves. British actors are inhibited about expressing their sexuality on stage and that's something I'm interested in: how do you stretch an actor sexually without making them vulnerable? I'm particular about historical details. How did a woman put on lipstick in the 1940s, for example? Period details have to be right.

Could you talk about the use of foreign languages in your work?
That's something that has grown with me. I love the sumptuousness of language. My grandmother was Rumanian, my father's side of the family were Lithuanians. I grew up used to hearing a lot of German and Yiddish. There are many languages going on in my head and I'm fascinated by the limitations that the speaking of just one language can impose. What happens beneath the logic of language in people? We all carry many different voices inside ourselves. In theatre it's a question of atmosphere again, of different melodies and rhythms that I want to explore; this is why I work with actors of different European nationalities.

Why is theatre important to you?
It's immediate. You can react to a political situation speedily and have something on stage in two to three weeks. The living experience of theatre is unique and remarkable, that chemistry between the actors and the spectators. Theatre is a place of risk, of debate and danger, as well as an aesthetic. I make theatre to provoke change rather than comfort the *status quo.* I align my practice with the German tradition. I like a practice which places high demands on the actor, which relies on minimal resources; to my mind there is nothing more interesting than the human body and the human voice.

At the moment physical theatre is fashionable in Britain but my interest in the physical and the linguistic comes from my cultural background and my training at E15 Acting School under Joan Littlewood, who was in turn influenced by Brecht.

Do you believe in a universal performance language?
No. There is no such thing as European theatre, only a theatre aesthetic which grows within individual cultural climates. As a director you might open up areas of taboo that the language you live in closes off. I work partly in France and the French culture for sexuality, food and wine opens up what is forbidden in a Protestant culture. In my practice I'm really trying to work in that realm of the 'child' before it is disciplined. If anything, I work for a language of sensuality, which is perfumed if you like; I work in the area of individual taboo which we deny or have squashed out of us.

Has your directing practice changed over the years?
I wanted to be a dancer and I worked as dance editor of *City Limits* for nine years. This had a profound effect on me and made me think about use of space and the way bodies work against each other. The ritual of Spanish and Indian dance interests me in particular. I learned a great deal through my training in ballet as a teenager and at drama school – its use of myth was something that has always intrigued me. We are steeped in myth.

I also develop a growing admiration for satire and vaudeville. I was influenced by the revues in the Blackpool tradition. I find that the use of the body in a non-naturalistic way comes into my directing again and again. There's a cabaret scene in the Holocaust trilogy when one of the female performers dances a routine with a Nazi cap as her partner. I wanted to show one country; France, lying down with another, Germany; so I took a vamp routine from vaudeville and made it a political act in a Brechtian sense. I like the Brecht/Weill routines too; the notion of music as a tool to disturb and titillate.

Who have acted as influences on you?
Louis Malle, the comedienne Hilda Baker, Claude Lanzmann, Punch and Judy. I like American writers like Dorothy Parker, Philip Roth and Mark Twain. Bruno Bettelheim's book *The Uses of Enchantment* had a seminal impact on me. I tend to think of everything I write or direct in terms of basic fairy-tale structure. *Theresa* became the Hansel and Gretel myth for me. I have also read the psychoanalyst Wilhelm Reich's work avidly; he theorizes that the body retains suppressed emotion and memories, and that pain is an expression of these. You have to lift self-censorship from actors. I always know that rehearsals are going well if the actors are telling sexy jokes. There is no morality on stage – though clearly as a director you have to be careful. It's especially hard for women performers to lose their conditioning, to want to please on stage. I look for the *Mensch* in my actors.

The Bible and biblical images play a big part in my work. I hung ladders from the ceiling in *The Dybbuk* (1992) and I know that I was thinking of Jacob's dream. There's so much brutality against women in the Bible, women are continually punished. I loved Merlin Stone's book *The Paradise Papers* and her history of the pre-Christian female goddesses and women prophetesses, her account of the taming of women through monotheism. I'm also haunted by the Queen of Sheba, the image of the black Jew. I think this may well be something that I will write about in the future.

In Britain I have been influenced by opera and ballet which both engage in large-scale visual scenarios that are often absent from so many text-based English productions. In Germany the theatre is less bound by text, and the visual, operatic qualities of staging are used as a form of 'bravura theatre'; I admire that.

What bearing does the audience have on your work?
I never write for a specific audience – that changes all the time anyway. Audiences differ regionally and it's interesting what different audiences carry with them. Doing a Holocaust play is a quite different experience in Germany than in Britain. When I adapted *Villette* (1996) I became interested in the struggle between Protestant and Catholic values but I didn't feel I was writing for a set of people that might be interested in those things too. As a writer I tell the audience things I think they should know. As a director I have a desire to tell a story and I'm attracted to writers who upset a certain norm. Right now I'm writing about the serial killer Henri Landru and I'm using the Bluebeard myth to connect with my audience.

Where do you see yourself in terms of a European directing landscape?
I think directing has always been conceived of as a male occupation. It's very tough to make your way as a woman director. You have to be clear-thinking, a manager of people and budgets – traditionally these are per-ceived as male attributes. I think I find it a greater challenge to be a writer-director; I love the journey into the unknown. Clearly, I straddle Europe. My work is multi-voiced, Jewish. Voices from the continent mix with voices from Britain and they inform each other. I'm not inter-ested in the directing hierarchy.

What preoccupies you as a director?
The idea of material poverty and intellectual, artistic richness. I read Grotowski at eighteen and the working of the mind, the musculation of the brain that performing forces you to do, fascinates me. If I had a lot of money I'd spend it on my actors, not on the décor.

My obsession is pushing the body beyond certain boundaries; to use the body to its maximum potential. Technology on stage leaves me cold, it's simply a fulfilment of machinery. It's frightening to push actors into areas of denial, to find the locked room inside an actor and force them to enter it. I'm constantly astonished by the amount of grief people carry inside them.

The liberations and restrictions of language will always have a grip on me as well. How do we express certain experiences through language? How do we translate emotion into words? This notion of translation was relevant in my Holocaust Trilogy and the damage that's been done to the second generation, the children of Jewish survivors. The sense of a double loyalty is one I feel keenly. I live here in England, but my ancestors came from Central Europe. We've all left other places behind; we all carry a medley of cultures within us.

Can you work as you want to in this country?
I've constructed my own working space. I'm outspoken. My experience with the Royal Shakespeare Company and the National Theatre confirmed my sense of the inequalities that exist in this profession for women. So I've founded my own company but lack of money restricts me a lot. The money is not there to support the level of the company's success. I have no separate space for the company and I work on a project basis. So I don't have the comforts of working in established theatre.

How would you like to develop as a director?
In Britain I have been influenced by opera and ballet which both engage in the large-scale visual scenarios that are absent from so many of our text-based productions. I'd like to work more with non-English-speaking actors. I like the bravura and the lack of inhibition in the continentals. There is no such thing as 'European' theatre, only a theatre aesthetic which grows within each cultural climate. In the German theatre aesthetic there is a particular fusion of the classical, modern and the political, and I admire this. In French productions, on the other hand, there is a concentration on 'spectacle', on the visual within a rhetorical style of delivery made at the cost of any political or philosophical interpretation. It is the modern German experimentation which fascinates me and it is in this direction that I am moving.

IAN SPINK

Born in Australia in 1947, Ian Spink began his career dancing with the Australian Ballet, Australian Dance Theatre and the Dance Company (New South Wales). Soon after his arrival in England in 1977 he formed the Ian Spink Group and started experimenting with dance theatre. In 1982 he co-founded Second Stride with Siobhan Davies and Richard Alston, and subsequently collaborated with designer/director Anthony McDonald and composer Orlando Gough. He has also collaborated extensively in opera, theatre and television. His recent work has included directing Judith Weir's *The Vanishing Bridegroom* (Scottish Opera, 1990), Donizetti's *Mary Stuart* (Scottish Opera-go-round, 1991), Handel's *Orlando* (Battignano Festival, Italy, 1992), Strindberg's *The Pelican* (Glasgow Citizens Theatre, 1992), Peter Handke's *The Hour We Knew Nothing of Each Other* (National Youth Dance Co., 1995) and Donizetti's *Daughter of the Regiment* (English Touring Opera, 1998). He also created movement for Caryl Churchill's *The Skriker* (Royal National Theatre, 1994), *Henry V* (Royal Shakespeare Company, Stratford, 1997), *The Tempest* (Royal Shakespeare Company, Stratford, 1998), *Eugene Onegin* (Opera North, 1998) and John Harle's *Angel Magick* (BBC Proms, 1998). Spink was Artistic Director of Second Stride until its closure in 1997 and he directed and choreographed twelve full-scale works for the company.

What is your principal medium?

There are four principal media for me: music, movement, text and image. I started training in ballet, and in my work something always seems to lead back to dance, music or movement. In this sense, my work tends to be a fusion of different forms where, for example, singers can be part of the action on stage. Since I've been working with designer/directors like Anthony McDonald, I've been exploring the kind of landscape in which theatre takes place, and the notion of the devised, visual landscape is becoming increasingly important to me. For a long time I've also been obsessed with using text; by this I don't mean mainstream theatre and the traditional play, I mean that I'm very interested in the idea of text itself and how it might be incorporated into a performance. My practice has mostly got to do with devising text, or lifting text from another source and recycling it. I'm particularly intrigued by the way that words can communicate certain things that movement or music can't. For instance, Second Stride did a piece a few years ago called *Bösendorfer Waltzes* which was initially an attempt to update *The Firebird* using new music by Orlando Gough. First of all, we explored the fairytale myths that had fed productions of that ballet in the early twentieth century. After that we started to look at the creative and visual arts scene in Europe around that time, especially the Dadaist and Surrealist movements. We had six performers and in the pre-rehearsal period we decided that each performer would investigate a famous Dadaist or Surrealist artist and would give a twenty-minute lecture in the style of that writer. Each of the six performers then went through the terrifying experience of giving this lecture in the style of these chosen historical figures, with the idea that we would incorporate parts of their lecture into the piece; this was finally rewritten by me as a performance text. In this situation I didn't perceive myself as a traditional writer, a playwright who'd written a play beforehand; instead I was part of the process. We've had other situations in which we had writers creating material that we improvised.

All my work goes through processes of transformation, and as a result it's very difficult to define a principal medium. Although I regard what I do as theatre, there is nothing really pure about it: my practice contains ideas and elements from different kinds of theatre. Sometimes the performance pieces I collaborate on have no text; for example, sometimes they contain very little dance. In my opinion the final production of a devised piece has a great deal to do with the people who are collaborating on it, and the collaborative process itself is akin to a relationship.

How would you define theatre/performance?
I find it difficult to define performance. I'd define theatre in the broadest possible sense and from a European perspective: it involves an audience who are watching an event which has been contrived to take place in front of them. Theatre can contain any of the elements of music, movement and text that I have just been discussing. If I were to describe the kind of theatre that I like, I would say that it's theatre that challenges, inspires and entertains; something that causes a reaction in the audience, perhaps even a sort of chemical reaction. Ballet is more about re-creation and repetition: when you go to a ballet you know what the story is beforehand, just as you do with a traditional opera. You enjoy it because you know what it's going to say; it is precisely the retelling that provides the enjoyment. I am interested in the kind of theatre where

you don't know what the story is, where you have to discover it. I'm interested in a theatre that breaks the rules, not that I believe I am creating anything new, but old ideas keep on resurfacing and we need to break away from them.

What are the guiding principles of your directing practice?
Gentle provocation and collaboration. I try to provoke people into responding to ideas, not aggressively but gently. I like working collaboratively and find conflict disturbing. I've recently been working with two people I've worked with before: a writer, Sian Evans, and a composer, Orlando Gough; we made a performance piece based on a novel called *Badenheim* by Aharon Appelfeld. The piece had fourteen performers who were a mixture of actors, musicians and dancers. Sian wrote the lyrics for the songs and Orlando composed the music for them. Sian also produced fragments of conversations, text, that the performers then acted, spoke and announced. We worked for a year or so on the structure and researched the novel, which is about a group of Jews in Austria who are just about to be relocated to Poland. We spent a lot of time researching that dreadful part of history. Together with the designer we assembled a cast and worked out a piece which was neither a play nor a film. It was not a naturalistic play in the sense that there were certain ideals and characters that were not represented in a naturalistic way, and in the fact that we were trying to tell the story through a multiplicity of narratives. I am aware of the European tradition that produces unorthodox plays like Peter Handke's *The Hour We Knew Nothing of Each Other*, which is completely silent, but there is a paucity of this kind of experimental theatre in Britain.

How do you work as a director?
Directors are really just manipulators of people, and their manipulation can be more or less subtle or aggressive. I prefer to be subtle. The art of direction is a process, a kind of collage of people and ideas. Although when I work I have an end vision, I also know that my vision is never going to be realized, and that it's a process that has got more to do with the way in which people operate, the way in which they create the finished thing. It is a process which includes the audience, and this is what makes every performance different from all others. Perhaps the difference in my work is that although there are roles, such as director, actor or writer, everybody can have a say in the process. The investment of the performers in the work is important to me: it's vital that people

understand what they are doing and that they have a connection with the work. I'm not the kind of director who walks in and says: 'This is the step that I want and you will emulate it exactly.' The most important thing when working with performers is that they own the material they are working on. Only in this way are they connected with it, and only then can they perform it with honesty and truth.

There certainly are times when I'm searching for something: when there is a sort of journey going on between me and the performer, or between me and the performance piece or my character. Often it isn't clear at the beginning where the end of the journey lies, and there can be a bit of deception surrounding the end of the journey. We have to be able to travel along a series of tracks before we find the right one. As a director I have to be able to give the performer confidence to go further. Sometimes that might mean that I have to try to coerce a performer into taking a number of different tracks. It's a kind of balancing act in that I have to try to keep all these possibilities in the air at the same time without rejecting any of them. I tend to find that going about this in a subtle way is the most effective means of achieving the solution.

Do you think there is such thing as a universal performance language?
I'm certainly not searching for one, and I don't think there is one. Different cultures have different languages of communication; only some aspects communicate to other cultures.

Has your notion of directing changed over the years?
Yes. I have to change as I experience work, otherwise I just fossilize. The changes I've undergone have to do with learning how other people approach things, especially performers; how actors work as opposed to dancers, or musicians. I've learned how they structure things in their heads and how they solve difficult tasks or problems. I increasingly learn that one doesn't actually have to do a lot while directing. I think I used to believe in doing everything, but actually it's the performers who have to do the performance. The director just has to find a way of triggering the performance to happen.

How does awareness of audience affect your work?
They are part of the world in which I live, and the work that I'm committed to needs an audience as part of its life. My kind of work is not universally popular. In fact it's not popular. I think some people find it difficult to watch it: they don't want to go through the groundwork. It is demanding, and people can become angry and disillusioned because

they expect dance and instead they get a lecture. In England, Second Stride have been trying to create the situation where we can have a dialogue with the audience afterwards. I think these question-and-answer sessions are very important as a way for us to get feedback from our audiences. My favourite audience response is when people have different ideas about what they have seen. At these times they themselves have become part of the creative process. Not that audiences aren't always part of the creative process, but my point is that if they can pick up different threads and combine them in their heads in different ways then I think it's a positive thing.

Who and what have acted as influences on your work?
I was particularly interested in ballet when I was younger. At that time eighteen-year-old Australian men were being conscripted to fight in Vietnam. The problem back then was that the language on stage had nothing to do with the political situation. It seemed to me that ballet was not the medium I should use if I wanted to express myself creatively. So I started choreography and learned contemporary dance techniques which at the time were hidden away in Australia. I came under the influence of American ideas and performers like Merce Cunningham and John Cage. Later I saw the work of Robert Wilson and Pina Bausch. I find Pina Bausch's emotional work shattering. I missed the seventies experimental theatre work, but I was aware that there was a lot of political theatre and dance happening in Britain and Europe. All these things have influenced me in different ways and have shown me that there are many different possibilities and avenues, and that's very inspiring. I've only mentioned the big names, the lighthouses, but I'm sure that many of these practitioners owe much to other practitioners whose names never get mentioned.

How do you see yourself in terms of the European theatrical/performance landscape?
I think I probably became absorbed into the English scene. When I first started working in London I was all for the Australian approach, which is quite rough and anti-establishment. My exposure to the system here is to a powerful class structure where the biggest theatre companies are on the whole run by men who have been to the right schools and the right universities, and that kind of theatre tends to attract the largest audiences and the most financial backing. There's a certain value in that work, but I feel happy to be outside it because it doesn't really allow me

to say what I want to say. I used to think that my work was more typical of the continent, but I increasingly think that this isn't the case. I probably became tainted by this country. I took on board many things, like a gentle way of working. My work isn't disturbing, unlike some work on the continent which is much more aggressive and unapologetic. Maybe this is why Second Stride hasn't actually toured a great deal in Europe.

Do you feel you can work as you want to work in this country?
I feel that I can work more easily in this country than I could work in Australia. Australia's theatre has developed in a different way from me. Much of its theatre looks to European work, and there's a reverence for anybody who comes from outside Australia. The same is true here for work that comes from the continent, but not to the same extent. The most interesting work in Australia is the pioneering work, and I don't see myself as a pioneer. As far as working in this country goes, I've been very lucky and I've had a lot of support. I can see that there are people who haven't been as lucky, whereas there have been times when I've been flavour of the month and I'm very grateful for that. On the other hand, funding is healthier in other countries and here there is a desperate lack of money in the arts because they are not considered to be important. Consequently, people have to fight harder; they've developed a siege mentality where you have to suffer and starve. This is not true for me. I'm old now. I don't see myself as being at the cutting edge of theatre or dance; in a way I've become 'respectable'. This has made things slightly easier.

What are your obsessions as a director?
In the role of director, which is a very powerful role, there is a moment during rehearsals where you are the most powerful person in the room. This is a situation where you have to expose yourself quite a lot and where you have to expose other people as well. My obsession is the attempt to create a happy, secure environment where this can happen. I think sometimes that this is not a good obsession. Sometimes the most interesting work is produced from creating situations which are unsafe, dangerous. There must be an aspect here where I'm trying to discover something about myself, or say something about myself. It seems I want to say something. I don't know what it is, but I'm desperately trying to say it somehow, and that's the situation in which I can say it. I don't know why I'm trying to say it through performance rather than through painting or writing.

What would you hope to see developing in terms of the director and their role in the next few years?

In Britain situations in which the performers or the makers of theatre are allowed to define what they do are rare. Most of the time situations are defined from the beginning and the director has to fulfil a role, the performer another role and so on. I think it would be good if there were more situations where people could actually go through the process of deciding how they work together or what their roles might be or how their roles might change. Of course this might come down to the fact that I think there ought to be more research and development into the way in which theatre is made. There is a vast group of people who fit into the slot and then get stuck in it. If you are working as an opera director, for example, you get hired by an opera company and they give you a cast of singers, their chosen opera, a conductor, an orchestra and a chorus, and you go in and try to bring the whole thing alive. But it existed already; the whole structure existed before you came along. This can be very dangerous because there isn't enough space to move, to create. All this needs to be investigated. At the moment it's often the smaller groups with no money which develop and create the most interesting ideas. It's these groups and these areas which should be encouraged. What I don't want is the situation where there are some theatre companies that get a lot of money, more buildings, spaces, studios and equipment, and a lot of others who eventually give up with broken hearts.

JATINDER VERMA

Born in Dar es Salaam, Tanzania, in 1954, Jatinder Verma lived in
Nairobi, Kenya, until 1968 when he moved to Britain. He studied History at the Universities of York and Sussex, and co-founded Tara Arts
with Sunil Saggar and Ovais Kadri in 1976. 'Tara' is the name of the
Celtic goddess of love and war, as well as that of a Buddhist goddess,
also of love and war (in Hindustani 'Tara' also means 'star'). Verma's
most notable productions with Tara Arts include: *Yes, Memsahib*
(1980), *The Broken Thigh* (1986), *Danton's Death* (1989), *Oedipus the
King* (1991), *Heer-Ranjha* (1992), *Troilus and Cressida* (1993), *Le Bourgeois Gentilhomme* (1994) and, for the Royal National Theatre, his own
adaptation of Molière's *Tartuffe* (1990) and Sudraka's eighth-century
Sanskrit classic *The Little Clay Cart* (1991).

What is your principal medium?
I am principally interested in a form of textual theatre which is strictly
linked with the body and music. Many would see this as a form of physical theatre, and I should say that I have difficulty with non-textual
physical theatre. Whenever I think of theatre, I think of a number of
interrelated areas such as song, music, the body and the voice. The
emphasis really is on the performer being as total a performer as is
humanly possible; by 'total' I mean the performer's capacity to be able
to shift effortlessly from a piece of dialogue into song, or into movement, to be able to slide from singing into acrobatics into acting. This
idea stems from the Indian notion of drama as consisting of movement,
costume, make-up, song and voice.

I cannot take on English, my main language of communication, without some severe dilemmas and questions, because my colonial history
makes English an 'adapted' language for me. This means that I can't just
take a play by Shakespeare and do it: there has to be some sense of a
commentary about and around the language itself. This is the origin of
my notion of 'binglish' which denotes the creation of a text which is not
quite in English.

How would you define theatre/performance?
Abhinava Gupta, a fourteenth-century Indian literary critic, said: 'Drama

is like a dream; it is not real, but it is really felt.' I agree with this view-point. As far as performance is concerned, I believe that it is a contract between those who are on the stage, or within the magic circle, and those who are watching. I think that this contract should be up front, one should never fight it. Therefore there ought to be all sorts of ways of breaking down the illusion of the audience's voyeuristic experience. If you honour your contract then you accept the fact that there is an audience watching you; you can talk directly to them or you can engage them in other ways. This contract between the performer and the audience must never be lost sight of.

In theatres which are popular in that they accept the populist and make use of whatever is around in their time and place to communicate and engage, conflict is a vital element of performance. In such theatre there is no notion of a fourth wall and the performers are constantly ready for any contingency; for instance, if someone coughs in the audi-ence the performers pick it up; if someone says something in the audi-ence they pick that up too. Both parties are engaged in the process. The audience knows that they can interfere with the performance and that the interference will not be rubbished or rejected. Even though we are still very far away from this kind of realization, I am absolutely sure that this is the way to go.

The truth of theatre is that it is unrepeatable and exists only in that particular moment and that particular context. The next day it might be the same performance but it would be another theatre, another rela-tionship; realizing the full truth of this means building a kind of impro-visatory text, or improvisatory space around the text. So far this has been achieved only to a limited extent, largely through music, especially Indian music, which by its very nature can't be fixed and always responds to the moment. Since music depends on who is playing it at a specific point of time, and since there is often more than one musician playing at the same time, music also depends on what the musicians feel towards each other. In this sense there is always a certain degree of improvisation taking place between the performer and the musician.

To give an example, in 1994 we did an adaptation of Molière's *Le Bourgeois Gentilhomme* where there were two lovers who mediated their love in terms of music. Our musician, Joji Hirota, accompanied them with a very basic four-beat Indian rhythm but one evening the actor began to sing to a seven-beat rhythm, so Joji quickly shifted to the same rhythm, which of course has another permutation made of fourteen beats. As he played along with the performer he then pushed it even further and went into a fourteen-beat rhythm, which is very slow. Now, one can ask oneself: who started this? Was it the actor or was it the musician? They both had to play along with each other's decisions and herewith reinvented the whole movement of the sequence. This is just one example of the variety of improvisation around live music, yet we are still one step away from the situation where a member of the audience intervenes in this fashion, which is the area into which I tend to move. I think ultimately I would like to work in a performance which is totally alive, where the sound, the smell, the sense of the people surrounding us are effectively part of the performance.

What are the guiding principles of your directing practice?
My guiding thought is that the actors are always better than me and that I therefore have to trust them implicitly. I suppose that's why I always work with the actors on the text before the rehearsals, so that they can reinvent the text and lend something of themselves to it. Finally, I believe that the company comes before the individual and that the company must be there at all times. The irony of this idea is that it is never achieved: the making of a company has to be worked at for each individual project. Although it is possible for me to assume that I might have achieved something definitive in this direction because I tend to work with the same performers, I find that in fact this is wrong: I have to start anew every time. Every time I do a standard exercise based on yoga called *surya-namasicar*, which means 'the creation of the sun'; I find it very effective for stretching the body and regulating the breathing. It's when the performers find complete relaxation through stillness and breathing that they begin to think of themselves as a company.

How do you work as a director?
I can't say that I'm a collaborator because the time always comes when the lie of this expression becomes evident in that I stop being in the same space as the actors and become a voyeur. My line of work facilitates the gradual empowerment of the actors and the disempowerment of myself in the hope that the actors become the possessors of their work and I simply become an observer. The more performances I direct, the more difficult I find it to write actors' notes, as the performers have an experience that I am no longer sharing with them.

As a director I try to be the 'other', the audience. Of course in a sense I will never really be able to 'be' the audience, but I like to think of myself as a kind of 'cynical other' who is waiting to be touched. So I could be described as a person who sets up certain conditions by which I expect to be emotionally moved.

In Tara we all share the dramaturgical work of research, rewritings and such like. I recently worked with my colleague from India, Anuradha Kapur, on *Cyrano*, which we transposed to a touring theatre company in India in the 1930s. I looked at the text, the spoken word, and she looked at the scenography. This distribution of roles has left me completely free to work on the text and its background. For six months Anuradha and I simply did all that, then the company became involved. The process of transposition brought us to question what theatre is and most of the answers have actually come out of the workshops that we did which involved things like character and movement, two elements that often equate in my work. Then we entered a new phase of the rehearsal period where I worked on gestures which told another kind of story and built up another kind of dialogue.

How do you differentiate yourself from other practitioners?
I find it difficult to make generalizations about the difference between my work and that of other directors because I've never followed other directors' work during the rehearsal period. I know that some directors have call sheets for individual actors, but I couldn't work without the whole company being there all the time. The idea that the whole company might not come together until the technical rehearsal is strange to me. I think the lack of ensemble work creates the 'luvvie syndrome' – which is when people go around saying: 'Oh, darling, how lovely to see you!', or 'Oh darling, you were wonderful!'

For me what matters is work that has resonance. Molière, for example, conjures a lyrical, even nostalgic atmosphere. This is almost at the heart of the Asian condition: the sentiment of going back home to a world somewhere else, a world that is lost, a life that was or still is epic. This is why adaptations have become an almost existential aspect of my work. Adaptations relate to my own life in that my life is an adapted life; my work represents an attempt to put some kind of order into chaos, into the fragments that make up my existence. Thus I am always conscious of fragments – snatches of song, snatches of another world colliding with snatches of this world. For me adapting a piece by Shakespeare means: 'I am having a dialogue with England.'

Adaptations have allowed Tara to contemporize the classics, not necessarily in terms of the setting or modern dress, but from the point of view of its debates, its problematics. There is a sort of nostalgia for a day that has gone, for the moment of time when creativity was a communal experience. Adaptations have also allowed us to pick out and touch upon contemporary sensibility. It has been six or seven years since we last did a contemporary play, and this is because I feel that our experience at this moment of time is of an epic kind and that's the text that I want. By epic, I mean shifting borders of nationality, understanding and asking what a nation is, what nationality is. This always demands a particular form of theatre that stretches into other media as well. For example, I am now working on something which is based on the incident that happened in Bow some years ago where a young Asian was so severely beaten by seven young thugs that his scalp hung off his skull. Subsequently one of the guys who beat him up was shopped by his girlfriend who is white. She was ostracized by her community and he ended up in prison, though not for very long. Circumstances forced the victim and the attacker's girlfriend to come together, and what came out was that the guy who'd beaten him up was himself half-Asian: now that's the state of England! This idea of 'shopping' made me think about shopkeepers, the main stereotype for Asians; and the whole notion of shopping. I'm now exploring this series of transactions. I don't want this to be yet another play about racism: I want this to be representative of a moment of transition in the country.

Do you think there is such thing as a universal performance language?
I have great trouble with the word universal because that word has enormous connotations for an ex-colonial. I grew up in Nairobi, Kenya, before independence and I grew up with notions of English meadows, English lawns, roses and daffodils. Then I witnessed independence and the beginning of the displacement of the English. So by now I am almost too conscious how over the past two or three hundred years that simple word 'universal' has led to the damnation of a huge range of other literatures. For a long time, the only way to understand one's own culture was by means of the other culture. Now we need to reacquire those lost, denigrated literatures. This is why I find 'universal' an almost impossible word to take on board. The only notion of universality I could entertain is in the context of what relates to different people in different times and different spaces. For instance, certain aspects of Noh theatre are very particular and they can relate to us in any time, in any place, and we can negotiate through its 'foreigness' to find the point where it touches us.

Has your notion of directing changed over the years?
I think I have changed. I have become much more conscious of how little I know. I suppose that I have become a bit more humble and a bit
more open to actors. I have lots of questions and few answers. I don't
know much. If you know everything, what point is there in doing anything? Yet even saying 'I don't know much' is not enough. So when I
say that I don't know much, I mean that we are all in the same boat and
that we all have to search for solutions.

How does awareness of audience affect your work?
It affects my work considerably. For instance, with *Cyrano*, Anuradha
Kapur and I have to keep in mind two sets of audiences because this
production is also going to India. She, of course, knows India much
more intimately than I do, so she thinks about the audience there and
tries to find out precisely what music to use, precisely what gestures,
whereas I am more conscious of the audience here. So there are details
that she is concerned about that I am not, because the audience here
wouldn't know enough about India for it to matter. For instance, there
is a point in the text where there is a sequence about food. I have chosen
a particular food which is *bindi*. Reading the text over there, she suggested another vegetable, which I agreed to. I only realized later that
the vegetable she suggested does not exist here and most of us don't eat
it here, whereas *bindi* is something people might remember from Indian
restaurants. Yet in other contexts those two sets of audiences are inter-
changeable in that a certain notion of Englishness would be understood
both here and over there, especially in the metropolitan cities whose
reality is bilingualism.

Who and what have acted as influences on your work?
The person who has most influenced my work is Anuradha Kapur of
whom I consider myself a kind of disciple. There are also certain productions that influenced me, such as Brian Friel's play *Translations*,
which I found brilliant for its use of language and notions of nationality.
Otherwise influences have come from traditional and modern theatre in
Asia: there is a kind of negotiation with modernity which I find inspiring and absolutely accurate for my own work. In that tradition I am
interested in ritual, not from a religious point of view but in the sense of
a performer who represents a moment of transition both for the performer and the audience.

How do you see yourself in terms of the European theatrical/performance landscape?
First of all I have to underline that this is a new Europe and since twenty-five million people who are not Europeans and yet live in Europe are not all of a sudden going to disappear from the European landscape, our inescapable destiny is that we have to redefine and reinvent the very concept of Europe. What characterizes the new Europe is that Africa and Asia are inextricably part of it, not only in terms of memory but also in terms of economy and capital.

Do you feel you can work as you want to work in this country?
I don't think anyone can work as they want, not just in this country, but in any country, at any time. We just have to try to make the work we want and that requires a certain degree of audacity, a great degree of luck, and a massive desire to do it, to want to fight. In this sense alone I can say that I have an enormous privilege, and that is being black in Britain. This forces you to look at things constantly and it forces you to struggle all the time. Even when you think you've been through everything, some idiot comes up to you and you think: 'Oh no! I have to explain myself yet again.' Being open also means that the main core of the work I do is the same. The details may change but the main core is there. In order to do this I have chosen theatre and not another medium because theatre is life. You can do with theatre things that no other medium can do. That's why I don't think that theatre will ever die.

What are your obsessions as a director?
My absolute obsession is migration and, of course, all that comes with it, such as transformation, cultural artifacts and signals, journeys, different spaces and times. In a sense my work is a comment on the notion of what is Asian. It's only since the 1980s that I have felt that the word Asian needs expansion; it has to incorporate the Japanese, the Chinese, the Burmese, the Indian and so on. I find myself going further and further east only to find that the notion of Asian is terribly elastic and touches a huge range of cultures.

I feel that as a director I have a responsibility in the sense that theatre is inherently didactic because it deals with symbols and we are constantly decoding those symbols. A sound gives you a signal, a word gives you a signal, a colour gives you a signal: all these are signals which could become questionable in certain circumstances. In a recent production of *Richard III* only the two murderers spoke in Glaswegian and Cockney, while the rest of the characters spoke a standard received pronunciation. What is the signal being given there about contemporary varieties of spoken English? No director can be oblivious to the play of such symbols today. Of course there is an extent to which we can't control how people decode the symbols we create but we must try to be conscious of the kinds of symbols we are working with; we must try to be conscious of what they say.

What would you hope to see developing in terms of the director and their role in the next few years?

I would like the director to return to the role of the actor-manager. I have a great deal of admiration for Simon McBurney in this respect. I also disagree with the idea that directors should be trained; I think that training courses take the director away from the company whereas in fact what is needed is the reverse. We also need new texts, new writing. For me writing for the theatre is never a lonely activity, it is a practical activity that takes place with the actors.

Deborah Warner

Born in 1959 in Oxford, Deborah Warner trained as a stage manager at the Central School of Speech and Drama from 1977 to 1979. In 1980 she founded her own group, Kick Theatre Company, of which she was Artistic Director until 1986. From 1987 to 1989 she was a resident director at the Royal Shakespeare Company, and since 1990 she has been an Associate Director at the Royal National Theatre. Her most notable productions include: *The Tempest* (Kick, 1983), *Measure for Measure* (Kick, 1984), *King Lear* (Kick, 1985), *Titus Andronicus* (Royal Shakespeare Company, 1987–8), *King John* (Royal Shakespeare Company, 1988), Sophocles' *Electra* (Royal Shakespeare Company, 1988–9), *The Good Person of Sichuan* (1989), *King Lear* (Royal National Theatre, 1990), Henrik Ibsen's *Hedda Gabler* (Abbey Theatre, Dublin and Playhouse Theatre, London, 1991), *Coriolan* (Salzburg Festspiele, 1993–4), Georg Büchner's *Wozzeck* (Opera North, 1993 and 1996), Samuel Beckett's *Footfalls* (Garrick Theatre, 1994), *Don Giovanni* (Glyndebourne, 1994–5), *Richard II* (Royal National Theatre, 1995–6), T. S. Eliot's *The Waste Land* (Brussels, Dublin, Paris, Toronto, Montreal, New York, London, 1995–8), *Une Maison de Poupée* (Odéon, Paris, 1997), Honegger's *St. Joan at the Stake* (BBC Proms, 1997) and *The Turn of the Screw* (Royal Opera House, 1997). In 1992 she was created a *Chevalier de l'Ordre des Arts et des Lettres* by the French government.

What is your principal medium?
Text-based theatre.

What characterizes your choice of texts?
I tend towards texts which, through their own ambition, depth and complexity, might be difficult or challenging to direct. I'm unlikely to be drawn to writers who don't seek to reveal something new, or to playwrights who think they know the shape of theatre. I'm also very excited by the possibilities of non-theatre text, and I'm particularly attracted to those classics which, like Tutankhamen's tomb, lie buried (often under the weight of a poor production history), waiting to be rediscovered.

If I weren't a theatre director I'd like to have been an explorer; in both jobs you set forth with a small group of people not knowing what you are going to find. No explorer would go somewhere that had already been discovered, or into territory that was known to be barren and unworthy of exploration.

Obviously one's collaborators have a big input into a choice of text. When I ran Kick I was heavily influenced by the casting possibilities within the company. More recently it was Fiona Shaw and my designer Hildegard Bechtler's enthusiasm for exploring *Hedda Gabler* that led us to the production for the Abbey Theatre (1991). I was not enthusiastic about directing *Hedda Gabler*, having seen many performances of the play, all of which seemed to merge into one monolithic interpretation. In fact I came to realize that I was confusing poor productions with the play itself. Thanks to Fiona and Hildegard's persistence we found a marvellous release mechanism within the Irish context, and to a great extent I believe we discovered a new play.

How do you see your role in the rehearsal room?

I can't accurately describe what takes place in the rehearsal room because it depends on what happens in front of me. This determines how I react and how I channel what I witness. Rehearsals are complex and organic processes which defy definition as much as they resist formal or intellectual structure. In text-based theatre the text, not, I believe, the rehearsal process, is the formal structure. My role is to create conditions for free exploration. I think it's correct to say that every actor needs to be directed differently, and it's certainly true that every beat must be approached quite separately. This is why it's always hard to give a description of rehearsals. It's like asking Picasso what he painted. If there is an answer, it lies in what he removed, scribbled out or painted over.

However, more often than not, I begin from an actor's idea rather than my own. This is because by the first day of rehearsals I have taken a lot of decisions already: I've named the play, cast the actors and probably, with the designer, designed the set. These decisions are enormous and likely to represent the most significant choices a director makes. So, from the moment of these choices to the moment when the piece is first shown to the public, I try to do my best to support the actors I have chosen and help them to shape their work. If I am after anything, it is the possibility of the performance 're-birthing' and engaging an audience night after night. For this possibility to exist, the process in the rehearsal room must be one of organic growth. The potential for true emotional expression must grow like a plant; it has to be able to put down its own roots. You can't force those roots, and if you do, the chances are that the roots will be weak and the plant will die. If the actors are not allowed the chance to find their own way or are asked to repeat, demonstrate or copy something, the performance will be dead – by which I mean it will appear false or boring. Quite simply, my role is to enable the organic process to happen so that the actors' performances can live.

What are the guiding principles of your directing practice?
Patience ought to be the guiding principle. Really good things don't happen fast. The other principle is bravery: to meet the actors' boundless bravery with one's own. Having a vision of the way ahead is fundamental; this mustn't be confused with 'having a concept', but is something rather like a well-trained hunting dog having a sense of direction, a sense of smell. Once a director and a group of actors are on this path, following their instincts, the real rehearsal process starts to happen. I never stifle a performer's ideas: I let the performance grow naturally. I am patient and wait for a glimmer of truth. Actors can't act truth: they have to be truth. That is the difficulty.

Do you think there is such thing as a universal performance language?
I think that there are universal emotions. If you communicate an emotional state powerfully, it will communicate to anybody in the world. I don't know what you mean by 'performance language', but I think that there are truths that can be communicated. I know that if a performer is honestly experiencing certain emotions, then these will necessarily communicate to other people.

How does awareness of audience affect your work?
I hope very much, since it's the audience that makes the theatre event. That's why the moment of the first performance is so important; because it is at that moment that the process begins and there is no going back. It's a loss of virginity. This makes the period before the first outing such a crucial time in the rehearsal process. During this phase of work I change gear. In the initial phase of the rehearsals I urge actors to try anything, use and explore everything; I keep quite quiet. In the run-up to the first performance I urge them to throw out irrelevant material and discard unhelpful experiences. I become very involved, very active. This often surprises actors I haven't worked with before, because up until that point they have felt very free, and then, suddenly, I urge them to follow one path rather than another. Of course in this way they will live to be free again, but for that moment they have to trust me absolutely.

Has your notion of directing changed over the years?

I hope that it is always changing. I think that I am more rigorous than when I began, perhaps because I am more aware of everyone's investment. I've learnt to structure my work better, by following a big project with a small one. For a long time I just did one big classic after another. I was repeating size, and that was a mistake. It's not always easy to get this balance right, but the nearest I got was *The Waste Land*, followed by *Richard II*, followed by *The St Pancras Project*, followed by *Don Giovanni*.

Who and what have acted as influences on your work?

Peter Brook has been an enormous influence. His vision of theatre, the way he runs his company, the productions themselves, all this has been very inspirational. When I was a child I saw his *Midsummer Night's Dream*, and as a student I saw *Ubu* and *The Cherry Orchard*. It was marvellous to see such great pieces of work at that age because they made me understand the potential of theatre. I am always troubled by students of theatre who can't answer when they're asked what great theatre they have seen. It makes me wonder where their belief in theatre comes from. Peter inspired me to trust in the form and illuminated the way brilliantly. In his writings, he has been able to articulate the invisible and the indefinable: to write about the essence of theatre in a non-intellectual, non-academic way. *The Empty Space* remains the best book written about the nature of theatre.

Fiona Shaw has been a great inspiration since I first worked with her on *Electra* in 1989. I feel privileged to have worked so closely with one of the most extraordinary, inspired and selfless actresses in Europe. She has made me trust in the supreme power of acting, and through her I have witnessed that acting can change people's lives.

I have also been grateful for anybody who challenges and redefines theatre. The list is long, but it must include Patrice Chéreau, Robert Lepage, Steven Berkoff, Ariane Mnouchkine and Peter Stein, to name but a few.

Could you elaborate on your interest in site-specific work?

The question of space lies at the heart of theatre. Choosing a theatre for a play is as fundamental as choosing an actor for a part. Any director exploring the nature of theatre will be involved in parallel research regarding space. 'Site-specific work' is an overused phrase which doesn't accurately describe my two boldest experiments with text and space.

The first of these, Samuel Beckett's *Footfalls*, started as an exercise in atmosphere and became an exploration of space. I chose the Garrick Theatre, which at the time lay somewhat forlorn and in need of repair, to explore Beckett's masterpiece of loneliness. The atmosphere of the dark theatre seemed a good starting-point. For the two-week rehearsal period I had the luxury of rehearsing with the actors in the theatre itself. That gave us the unique possibility of rehearsing in order to find the place within the building that most released the play. The building was the set and how we used it was our journey. The organization of theatrical space is mainly concerned with the placing of the audience. Our expectation of proscenium arch theatre is that we know where the audience will be. In *Footfalls* (1994) we found that the central character, May, shouldn't inhabit the stage, but the space beneath the gallery and the front of the dress circle, with the stucco plaster work of the gallery bearing down on her head. The audience were in the stalls and had to turn round and look up to see her. Sadly, the Beckett estate overreacted badly at this new aesthetic departure, but it released the play magnificently.

The Waste Land (1995–6), a recital of the poem by T. S. Eliot, performed by Fiona Shaw in a series of carefully chosen non-theatre spaces, has also been revealing in terms of the combustion of non-theatre text with non-theatre space. We have played in buildings ranging from a disused gunpowder store in Dublin, to a life-drawing classroom in the École des Beaux Arts in Paris, to an abandoned industrial site in Toronto, to an empty cinema in Montreal. As we talk, this journey is still continuing, so I couldn't say exactly what I've learned, but I've been truly challenged as far as staging techniques are concerned.

What role did the St Pancras project play within this kind of experimentation?
St Pancras was my first journey into non-text-based theatre. I was commissioned by LIFT (the London International Festival of Theatre) to create an on-site event in a London building. I chose the remarkable Midland Hotel above St Pancras's railway station. Built in the 1870s by Gilbert Scott, the hotel was closed at the turn of the century, and then enjoyed various lives as British Rail offices, until its final complete closure and abandonment in the 1970s. As it stands, it awaits its fate, in need of substantial repair, but boasting great beauty and an extraordinary atmosphere caught as it is between lives.

LIFT's commission to me was generously open: I could do 'as I liked' with the building. I began the project by thinking that I would find (or write) a text and discover a way of putting the text and its audience into the building. But the more I tried to think of a text, the less I could find one. Eventually, I realized that the true text was the silent one of the building itself. As I began to think how the audience could receive the building, I realized that what was unique and thrilling about my experience was that I was visiting it alone. The strange power of being alone in this vast silent labyrinth of corridors on the corner of the Euston Road was overpowering. I had to try to find a way for the audience to have a similar experience. The finished project was a walk: the audience were invited to enter the building one at the time at ten-minute intervals, and they were asked to follow a painted line about a mile long which took them from the bottom to the top of the building. The walk was enhanced by my designer, Hildegard Bechtler, and six performers were employed, who appeared like fleeting ghosts in this haunting or dream.

The project prompted a series of questions about the role of the director and the nature of theatre. What did the director do? Who supplied the text? Who was the performer? Who was the audience? It was a fascinating experience which Kate Kellaway from the *Observer* described as being 'in one's own poem'.

How would you define theatre and performance?
I suppose theatre is an organized event with performance at its centre. I have much more trouble defining performance. I think it is an attempt by an individual or a group of individuals to animate the space that lies between themselves and the audience. Some would argue that this space is always alive, in which case I would say that it is an attempt not to kill this space!

The question of how we define theatre is becoming increasingly important to me. Every time I make a new work I'm trying to define theatre. Perhaps I wouldn't do theatre if I knew exactly what it was.

Do you feel that you can work as you want to work in this country?
Not always, but I am very lucky to have strong connections with continental Europe which can sometimes supply the missing link. Claire Bejanin and Ariel Goldenburg from the Théâtre de Bobigny in Paris were financially and creatively responsible for *Footfalls*. Frei Leysen and the Kunsten Festival des Arts in Brussels funded *The Waste Land*. These projects would probably not have happened otherwise.

What would you hope to see developing in terms of the director in the future?
I would like to see a restructuring of our funding system. The French

traditionally fund the artist as opposed to the building, and I would like us to follow this model. Currently we have admirable buildings with less than admirable work in them, and that is becoming a problem. When theatrical exploration needs to happen outside our theatre buildings it is often very difficult to attract funding. This doesn't mean that I don't believe in the Royal National Theatre or the Royal Shakespeare Company. I believe in them passionately, but we must be flexible in our funding. This is a very delicate subject these days, when criticism of any institution is taken as a reason to close it down.

I would also like to see theatre critics inspire the theatre rather than hold it back by a dreary relationship to what constitutes a theatrical event and what doesn't.

THE COMING OF THE THIRD MILLENNIUM

Popular version of the
Apostolic Letter of Pope John Paul II
Tertio Millennio Adveniente
on the Jubilee of the Year 2000

CAFOD/SCIAF/TRÓCAIRE/MISSIONARY SOCIETY OF ST COLUMBAN

Original text:	CEAS and Mateo Garr SJ
Drawings:	Ricardo Zegarra
Translation:	Ed O'Connell SSC
Adaptation:	Ed O'Connell SSC and Brian Davies
Editing:	Ellen Teague

© 1996: Missionary Society of St Columban
ISBN: 1 871549 56 6

Published June 1996
Fourth Printing November 1996

Missionary Society of St Columban
Widney Manor Rd   Dalgan Park
Knowle   Navan
Solihull   Meath
West Midlands B93 9AB   Ireland
01564 772096   353 46 21525

CAFOD   SCIAF
Romero Close   Scottish Catholic International Aid Fu■
Stockwell Rd   5 Oswald St
London SW9 9TY   Glasgow G1 4QR
0171 733 7900   0141 221 4447

TROCAIRE
169 Booterstown Avenue
Blackrock
Co. Dublin
Ireland
353 1 288 5385

In collaboration with:

National Liaison Committee of Diocesan Justice and Peace Groups of Engla■
and Wales
38-40 Eccleston Square
London SW1V 1BX
0171 834 8550

Justice and Peace Scotland   The Irish Commission for Justice and Pe■
65 Bath Street   169 Booterstown Avenue
Glasgow G2 2BX   Co Dublin, Ireland
0141 333 0238   353 1 288 5021

Printed by Abacus Printing Co Limited London EC1R 0BN

CONTENTS

PREFACE

In November 1994 Pope John Paul II wrote an Apostolic Letter concerning the preparation for the year 2000. It will be a great Jubilee celebration for all the Church.

In the Old Testament we learn about the years of Jubilee. They were a time of liberation and of God's favour. In the same way, when Jesus began his public ministry he announced a Jubilee for the poor. It is with this same spirit that we wish to celebrate the Jubilee of the Year 2000 and to reflect about the themes of Justice, Reconciliation and Unity among Christians.

To help us in this reflection, a popular version of the Pope's letter has been prepared by those working on the Millennium: Missionary Society of St Columban, CAFOD, SCIAF, and TRÓCAIRE. The text is based on a popular version produced by CEAS, the Peruvian Episcopal Commission for Social Action, and we are grateful for permission from CEAS to re-work their original summary.

We hope that this new publication will assist the whole Church in:

* acknowledging past wrongs;
* knowing more about the Social Teaching of the Church and the work of the Second Vatican Council;
* promoting changes to be made in favour of the poor and excluded;
* renewing our commitment to Christian Unity.

Bishop John Crowley
Chairman, CAFOD

Bishop John Aloysius Mone
Chairman, SCIAF

Bishop John Kirby
Chairman, TRÓCAIRE

Very Rev Nicholas Murray
Superior General, Missionary Society of St Columban

INTRODUCTION

In less than four years we will reach the year 2000.
The beginning of that year is going to be very special:
Not only will it be a new year
and a new **century**,
but also a new **millennium**.

A **millennium** means 1000 years.
With the year 2000, we end two millennia
and we begin the third millennium.

1. What happened 2000 years ago?

Why did the calendars start then?

According to tradition Jesus was born nearly 2000 years ago,
although we do not know the exact date.
Many centuries ago, people decided to start the calendar
with the birth of Jesus.

About 2000 years ago Jesus was born in Bethlehem.
He lived for little more than 30 years in Palestine.
He died on a cross in Jerusalem, rose again from the dead
and ascended into heaven.

9

This most important event of history
is what we call the *Redemptive Incarnation of Jesus*
(paragraph 1).

It is our custom to celebrate anniversaries
and this is the most important one of all.

2. The Jubilee of the year 2000

In the Church special anniversaries
are called JUBILEES.
Jubilee has come to mean Joy.
We are going to celebrate the Jubilee Year 2000.

Like all anniversaries
we have to prepare well for this Jubilee.
It will be celebrated throughout the world.

To help us prepare for the Jubilee
Pope John Paul ll has written a letter.
It is an *Apostolic Letter*
written to the whole Church.

Like all the official letters written by the Pope,
it is known by its opening words in Latin,
the original language of the Church.

In Latin the Apostolic Letter is called
Tertio Millennio Adveniente
which means
The Coming of the Third Millennium.

John Paul II published this letter on 10 November 1994.

In the letter John Paul II invites us
to prepare for the Jubilee Year 2000
and puts before us many things that we can do
so that this very important event
is a true celebration of our faith.

3. How to study the text

As his letter *Tertio Millennio Adveniente* is important
we have prepared this **popular version**
so as to put the contents at the service
of the Christian community in this country.

A **popular version** is a **summary** of the text
in a language that is simple and easy to understand
with questions to guide us in our learning.
When we quote the exact words of the letter
we will use this type of lettering (italic)
and indicate the number of the paragraph in the original
   text.
The sections within each chapter are numbered.
These numbers do NOT appear in the original text
but are for the convenience of readers.
The summary will be presented in normal lettering.

As this is a long document,
do not try to read it all at one time.
It is better to read it in parts.

It will be even better to look at it in groups:
— take a section
— each person read it quietly
— then let someone read it aloud for all.

— Does everybody understand it?

— You have to understand the text if you want to work on it.
— Maybe you want to read it a few times over so that all will
      understand it.
— Afterwards, respond to the questions that are there for
      each section.

Hopefully, this **popular version** will help you
understand the message of Pope John Paul II,
so that you can prepare your own Christian community
for the Jubilee Year 2000.

1

"JESUS CHRIST IS THE SAME YESTERDAY AND TODAY..."

(paragraphs 1-8)

John Paul II begins his letter by reminding us
that God sent his Son into this world.
What we celebrate in the Jubilee
is this mystery of the Incarnation of Jesus Christ:

*The fact that in the fullness of time the Eternal Word
took on the condition of a creature
gives a unique cosmic value to the event
which took place in Bethlehem two thousand years ago.
(paragraph 3)*

The Son of God became man;
he has sent us his Spirit
and now all of us are sons and daughters of God.

1. The history of the Incarnation

We all know the history of the Incarnation:
In the Midnight Mass at Christmas
we listen to the Gospel of St Luke (Lk 2:1-7)
that tells us of the birth of Jesus.
In the previous chapter of St Luke we are told
of the Annunciation to Mary by the Angel (Lk 1:26-28).
Never in the history of the world
has so much depended on the decision of one person.

St John relates the same in his Gospel (Jn 1:14):

And the Word became flesh
and dwelt among us,
full of grace and truth;
we have beheld his glory,
glory as of the only Son from the Father.
(paragraph 3)

Also St Paul speaks about Christ
in his letter to the Colossians (Col 1:15):

He is the first born of all creation. (paragraph 3)

2. The Effects of the Incarnation

When he was born in Bethlehem
Jesus made us his brothers and sisters
and renewed all of creation.
Christ....is therefore
the one who reveals God's plan
for all creation,
and for human beings in particular.
In the memorable phrase
of the Second Vatican Council,
"Christ fully reveals the human person
and makes our supreme calling clear." (paragraph 4)

The document which John Paul II quotes
is the Pastoral Constitution *Gaudium et Spes*
on the Church in the Modern World, paragraph 22.

13

This is what gives us our dignity as human beings.
The Pope says:
By his incarnation the Son of God
united himself in some sense with every person...
and, sin apart, he was like us in every way. (paragraph 4)

As Jesus was born in such a humble way,
the great people of the time did not know about it.
All that we know about the person of Jesus
comes from the pages of the New Testament.

3. God speaks to us

In the times before Jesus
God spoke to his people through the prophets.
For us Christians
the Old Testament brings us to Christ.

In the fullness of time
God speaks to us directly through his Son.

"In many and various ways
God spoke of old to our fathers by the prophets;
but in these last days he has spoken to us by a Son"
(Heb 1:1-2). (paragraph 5)

This is what is special about our Christian faith:

It is not simply a case of us seeking God,
but of God who comes in Person to speak to us
about himself
and show us the path
by which he may be reached.
(paragraph 6)

Jesus Christ is not only the Word
of God that speaks to us.
Jesus Christ is also our answer to God.
And not only our answer to God
but the answer of all creation also.
In St Paul's letter to the Ephesians (Eph 1:10)

he says to us that
Jesus Christ is the recapitulation of everything. (paragraph 6)

As human beings
we form part of all creation.
St Irenaeus says to us that
the glory of God can be seen in the fact that we are alive.

4. *God seeks us out*

In Jesus Christ God not only speaks to us
but also seeks us out. *(paragraph 7)*

Remember the parable of the lost sheep?
St Luke tells us the parable in 15:1-7.
Although God redeemed all creation
it is only us human beings that God
named as his adopted sons and daughters.

If God seeks us out in Christ
it is because we have been lost.
Like our first parents Adam and Eve
we have preferred the path to evil.
But Jesus came to overcome evil:
*Overcoming evil: this is the meaning of the Redemption.
(paragraph 7)*
He has reconciled us to the Father
by his death on the cross.

Our religion is not only that of the Incarnation
but also of the Redemption.
Now we participate in the same life of God.
*The religion which originates
in the mystery of the Redemptive Incarnation,
is the religion of "dwelling in the heart of God",
of sharing in God's very life. (paragraph 8)*

As St Paul says in his letter to the Galatians (Gal. 4:6):
*God has sent the Spirit of his Son into our hearts,
crying, Abba! Father! (paragraph 8)*

15

QUESTIONS
to help us understand the text

In all of this chapter of introduction
Pope John Paul ll has summarised
what we call "the history of salvation".
God speaks to us in Jesus Christ
and seeks us in Jesus Christ.

How does Christ speak to us today?
Through whom does he speak to us?

How does Christ seek us out today?
In what situations or events does he seek us out?

The Pope speaks to us of the Incarnation of Christ
    and also of the Redemption which Christ brought about.
How do we explain what these mean
    to our children, students and friends?

Do we believe that the life of Jesus Christ
    is the most important event in all history?
What does the life of Jesus Christ mean for our own
    history?

How do we demonstrate our faith in practice?

2

The Jubilee of the year **2000**

(paragraphs 9-16)

1. God has entered into our time

Never has such a thing happened in history:
Eternity entered into time. *(paragraph 9)*

Only in the Christian faith
do people believe that eternity comes to us.
Christ comes to meet us.

If we meet with God in this life
then we begin
to live our destiny on the earth:

People achieve this fulfilment of their destiny
through the sincere gift of self:
a gift which is made possible only through their encounter with God.
It is in God that people find full self-realisation.
This is the truth revealed by Christ.
People are fulfilled in God,
who comes to meet him through the Eternal Son. (paragraph 9)

Our time meets with eternity.

It is not that we go outside of time,
rather that God enters into our time.
Before the arrival of Jesus,
the people of Israel lived in expectation.
Now that Christ has arrived,
we live in the time of fulfilment.

In Jesus Christ, the Word made flesh,
time becomes a dimension of God,
who is eternal. (paragraph 10)

2. Our time is holy

Just as the eternal God has entered into time
we must make time holy.
We must sanctify time.

Remember the Easter Vigil,
how the paschal candle is marked
with the numerals of the current year,
equally in the liturgical calendar
we are reminded that each year,
each day,
each moment
reproduces the whole mystery
of the Incarnation and Redemption. (paragraph 10)

3. What is a jubilee?

To know what the Jubilee is,
let us read the text of Luke 4:16-21:

Jesus of Nazareth,
going back one day to the synagogue of his home town,
stood up to read.
Taking the scroll of the Prophet Isaiah,
he read this passage (Is 61:1-2):
The Spirit of the Lord has been given to me,
for he has anointed me.

He has sent me to bring the good news to the poor,
to proclaim liberty to captives,
and to the blind new sight,
to set the downtrodden free,
to proclaim the Lord's year of favour.
He then rolled up the scroll,
gave it back to the assistant and sat down.
And all eyes on the synagogue were fixed on him.
Then he began to speak to them:
"This text is being fulfilled today even as you listen."
(paragraph 11)

Jesus reminds us of a custom
which began in the Old Testament:
he announced *the Lord's year of favour.*
This is what JUBILEE means.

The Jubilee is the fullness of time.
This is when salvation arrives;
when the Messiah comes,
the Christ:
It is he who proclaims the good news to the poor.
It is he who brings liberty to those deprived of it,
who frees the oppressed
and gives back sight to the blind. (Mt 11:4-5; Lk 7:22)
In this way he ushers in
"a year of the Lord's favour",
which he proclaims not only with his words
but above all by his actions.
The Jubilee, "a year of the Lord's favour",
characterises all the activity of Jesus;
it is not merely the recurrence of an anniversary in time.
(paragraph 11)

In Jesus all the Jubilees of the Old Testament
had reached perfection.

4. How was the Jubilee celebrated in the Old Testament?

In the times of the Old Testament

the Jubilees were celebrated every seven years,
for that reason they are also called "sabbatical years".
Every seven years
slaves were freed and debts cancelled.
If you wish to know more about this,
read the Book of Exodus 23:10-11;
the Book of Leviticus 25:1-18;
and the Book of Deuteronomy 15:1-6.

After seven sabbatical years,
that is in the fiftieth year,
there was a special celebration of JUBILEE.
(Read the Book of Leviticus 25:10.)

One of the most significant consequences
of the jubilee year
was the general "emancipation"
of all the dwellers on the land in need of being freed....
They could never be completely deprived of land,
because it belonged to God;
nor could the Israelites remain forever
in a state of slavery,
since God had "redeemed" them for himself
as his exclusive possession
by freeing them from slavery in Egypt. (paragraph 12)

Unfortunately,
this legislation was more an ideal than a reality;
but nevertheless
a kind of social doctrine began to emerge
which would then more clearly develop
beginning with the New Testament.
The jubilee year was meant to restore equality
among all the children of Israel. (paragraph 13)
The poor would reclaim their property
and the rich would have to recognise
the rights of the poor.

In this way justice would be done
and the weak would be protected.
God alone is the Lord of all Creation.
If in his Providence

God had given the earth to humanity,
that meant that he had given it to everyone.
Therefore the riches of Creation
were to be considered as a common good
of the whole of humanity....
The jubilee year was meant to restore this social justice.
(paragraph 13)

5. The Jubilee and the social doctrine of the Church

The social doctrine of the Church,
which has always been a part of Church teaching
and which has developed greatly in the last century,
particularly after the encyclical Rerum Novarum,
is rooted in the tradition of the jubilee year. (paragraph 13)

So, for this reason, the Jubilee is a year of the Lord's favour:
a year of the remission of sins
and of the punishments due to them,
a year of reconciliation between disputing parties,
a year of manifold conversions
and of sacramental and extra-sacramental penance.
(paragraph 14)

6. The Jubilees in our lives

Each one of us
celebrates jubilees in our personal lives,
for example, when we celebrate birthdays.
We also celebrate religious jubilees,
for example, when a couple
celebrate their silver wedding anniversary
or when a priest celebrates
the anniversary of his ordination.

Also, institutions celebrate jubilees,
for example, a city or a parish
celebrates the anniversary of its foundation.

In view of this,
the two thousand years which have passed since the Birth of
  Christ...

represent an extraordinarily great Jubilee,
not only for Christians
but indirectly for the whole of humanity,
given the prominent role played by Christianity
during these two millennia. (paragraph 15)

The Jubilee means joy
in the hearts of each person.
In the same way the activity of Christ
was a Jubilee for the people of his time.

This indicates that the Church
rejoices in salvation.
She invites everyone to rejoice,
and she tries to create conditions
to ensure that the power of salvation
may be shared by all. (paragraph 16)

Of all the Jubilees which have been celebrated
down through history,
the Jubilee of the Year 2000
will be one of the greatest.

In this spirit the Church rejoices,
gives thanks
and asks forgiveness,
presenting her petitions to the Lord of history
and of human consciences. (paragraph 16)

7. The unity of Christians

One of the principal prayers of the Church
is for the unity of all Christians.
That which unites us is more important
than that which separates us.
It will be good if the Jubilee could be celebrated ecumenically.
In this way the Jubilee will bear witness
even more forcefully before the world
that the disciples of Christ
are fully resolved to reach full unity as soon as possible
in the certainty that "nothing is impossible with God".
(paragraph 16)

QUESTIONS
to help us understand the text

In this chapter the Pope has explained
what a Jubilee means
and what its biblical sources are.

Each of us can think of some examples
   of **personal** jubilees that we celebrate.
What **community** jubilees do we celebrate?
What **religious** jubilees do we celebrate?

How do we celebrate these jubilees?

Let us read once more Luke 4:18-19:
He has sent me to bring the good news to the poor,
to proclaim liberty to captives,
and to the blind new sight,
to set the downtrodden free,
to proclaim the Lord's year of favour. (paragraph 11)

This "year of favour" or Jubilee
characterises all the activity of Jesus.

This being so, then if Jesus is acting in this way today in
   our world:

Who needs to hear this message?
What would be "good news" to the poor?
Who are the blind who need to see?
Who are the "downtrodden" today and what do they
   need to be freed from?
How do we proclaim the Jubilee today?
What would a Jubilee mean for developing countries
   today?

3

PREPARATION FOR THE GREAT JUBILEE

(paragraphs 17-28)

In the Church's history
every jubilee is prepared for
by Divine Providence. (paragraph 17)

In each period of history
we ask ourselves about God's action:
In what way has God acted in our history,
in the last 1000 years
and, above all, in the twentieth century?
We celebrate this presence with gratitude.

1. We are celebrating the Second Vatican Council

As Catholics,
the most important event of this century
has been the Second Vatican Council.
This Council was different from those that went before it
because it was a Council
focused on the mystery of Christ
and his Church
and at the same time open to the world. (paragraph 18)

The Second Vatican Council
is often considered as the beginning of a new era
in the life of the Church. (paragraph 18)

The Council brought together
the best of the old and the new.

The Vatican Council opened the way
for the Jubilee of the year 2000
because it was a preparation
of that new springtime of Christian life
which will be revealed by the Great Jubilee. (paragraph 18)

2. The Council was like John the Baptist

Remember what St Luke says (3:1-7)
when speaking of John the Baptist.
The Council was like the prophet John:
because it showed to the world the *"Lamb of God*
who takes away the sin of the world" (John 1:29) (paragraph 19)
and invites all people to conversion.

The bishops in meeting at the Council
wrote sixteen documents about diverse themes.
Amongst the most important
they spoke about the identity of the Church,
the Word of God,
the reform of the liturgy
and the Church in the Modern World.

No Council has ever spoken so clearly
about Christian unity,
about dialogue with non-Christian religions,
about the specific meaning of the Old Covenant and of Israel,
about the dignity of each person's conscience,
about the principle of religious liberty,
about the different cultural traditions
within which the Church carries out her missionary mandate,
and about the means of social communication. (paragraph 19)

3. The Council was like the Sermon on the Mount

The Council spoke in the language of the Gospel,
the language of the Sermon on the Mount and the Beatitudes.
In the Council's message
God is presented in absolute Lordship over all things,
but also as the One who ensures
the authentic autonomy of earthly realities....
It was with the Second Vatican Council that,
in the broadest sense of the term,
the immediate preparations for
the Great Jubilee of the Year 2000
were really begun. (paragraph 20)

That being so,
the best preparation
for the Jubilee
is to apply the teachings of the Council
to our lives and the life of the Church.

Just as the liturgical time of Advent
is the preparation for the coming of Christ
who will always come (Rev 4:8),
so also the Council is like
the Advent of the Great Jubilee.

4. The Synods (Meetings) of the Bishops

In the 30 years that have followed the end of the Council
other important events have occurred:

There have been a series of Synods
begun after the Second Vatican Council:
general Synods together with
continental, regional, national and diocesan Synods.

One of the most important was in 1974
on the theme of Evangelisation.
The Synods have also spoken about
justice in the world,
the mission of the laity,
the formation of priests,

catechesis,
the family,
penance and reconciliation,
and consecrated life.
The Synods helped to prepare us for the Jubilee.

The preparation for the Jubilee Year 2000
is thus taking place throughout the whole Church,
on the universal and local levels,
giving her a new awareness of the salvific mission
she has received from Christ. (paragraph 21)

5. The letters of the Popes

All the Popes of the past century
have prepared for this Jubilee....
Furthermore, in the course of this century the Popes,
following in the footsteps of Leo XIII,
systematically developed
the themes of Catholic social doctrine. (paragraph 22)

From 1891 when Pope Leo XIII
wrote the encyclical *Rerum Novarum*
(which means "Of New Things")
the Popes have dedicated themselves
to announce the Good News on human work.

In 1931 Pius Xl wrote *Quadragesimo Anno*
(which means "In the fortieth year");

in 1961 John XXIII wrote *Mater et Magistra*
(which means "Mother and Teacher");

in 1971 Paul VI wrote *Octogesima Adveniens*
(which means "Nearing the eightieth year").

The present Pope, John Paul II,
has written two encyclicals about work:

in 1981 *Laborem Exercens*
(which means "The Exercise of Work")

and in 1991, on the 100th anniversary of *Rerum Novarum,*
he wrote *Centesimus Annus*
(which means, "In the 100 Years").

There have also been letters written about peace and developm●
John XXIII wrote *Pacem in Terris* in 1963
(which means "Peace on Earth").

Paul VI wrote *Populorum Progressio* in 1967
(which means, "The Development of Peoples").

John Paul II wrote *Sollicitudo Rei Socialis* in 1987
(which means, "The Social Concern of the Church").
(paragraph 22)

Two themes that repeat themselves
throughout all the encyclicals
are the dignity and rights of human beings
and the promotion of peace.

The theme of Jubilee also repeats itself
through all the writing of John Paul II.

It is aimed at an increased sensitivity
to all that the Spirit is saying
to the Church and to the Churches (Rev 2:7),
as well as to individuals through charisms
meant to serve the whole community.
The purpose is to emphasise what the Spirit
is suggesting to the different communities,
from the smallest ones, such as the family,
to the largest ones, such as nations
and international organisations,
taking into account cultures, societies and sound traditions.
(paragraph 23)

6. The papal journeys of John Paul ll

To see that the teachings of the Council are applied,
John Paul II not only wrote encyclicals.
He has also undertaken many journeys.

John Paul II has visited Churches
in all the continents:
Europe and America,
Asia and Africa.

Papal journeys have become a regular occurrence,
taking in the particular Churches in every continent
and showing concern for the development of ecumenical relationships
with Christians of various denominations. (paragraph 24)

7. Celebrating the Jubilee locally

In preparing for the Year 2000,
the individual Churches have their own role to play,
as they celebrate with their own Jubilees
significant stages in the salvation history
of the various peoples. (paragraph 25)

8. The celebration of the Holy Years

Another way in which preparation
has been made for the coming of the Jubilee Year 2000
has been the Holy Years.
Paul VI called one in 1975
and John Paul II another in 1983,
remembering the 1950 years
since the death of our redeemer Jesus.
There was another between 1987 and 1988
in honour of Mary, the mother of Jesus,
celebrating *the presence of the mother of God*
in the mystery of Christ and the Church. (paragraph 26)

It would be difficult not to recall
how the Marian Year occurred
shortly before the events of 1989
when there was a *peaceful resolution*
of the crisis of the socialist countries.

Tragically, peace does not exist
in all of these countries:
In the countries of the former Eastern bloc,
after the fall of Communism,
there appeared the serious threat

29

of exaggerated nationalism,
as is evident from events in the Balkans
and other neighbouring areas. (paragraph 27)

9. The Jubilee and families

Each family should in some way be involved
in the preparation for the Great Jubilee.
Was it not through a family,
the family of Nazareth,
that the Son of Man chose
to enter into human history? (paragraph 28)

QUESTIONS
to help us understand the text

In this chapter we have read
about the preparations for the Jubilee
during recent decades.
The principal ecclesial event in this century
was the Second Vatican Council
which was held in Rome during the 1960s.
There have also been Synods of bishops,
meetings of the local churches in each continent
and journeys by Pope John Paul II.

Just as John the Baptist announced Christ,
so these meetings and declarations
are an announcement of the Jubilee Year 2000.

What do members of your community remember about
the Second Vatican Council?
How has the life of the Church changed since the Vatican
Council?

What do you know about the contents of the social
encyclicals?
How could you find out more about the Church's social
teaching?
What does it say to our world today?

What do you remember about the Pope's visit to your
country?

Have there been any national gatherings of the Church in
your country which have have been particularly
influential?
(Some examples might be:
The National Pastoral Congress of England and Wales in
1980,
"The Challenge of the Nineties: The Church in the Heart
of the World" gathering in Scotland in 1992.)

4

IMMEDIATE PREPARATION
A) FIRST PHASE 1994-1996

(paragraphs 29-38)

The Holy Father John Paul II proposes
a specific programme of initiatives
for the immediate preparation of the Great Jubilee. (paragraph

To make possible a programme for the whole world,
it has been necessary to consult
all those responsible for the local churches,
and in particular all the Cardinals of the Church.

1. Two Phases of preparation
1994 - 1996 and 1997 - 1999

A first suggestion has been
to divide the preparation into two parts:
first will come the general awareness raising during the years *1.*
    96: this will be the *First Phase.*

The Second Phase will be the intensive preparation

during the years *1997, 1998* and *1999.*

2. The First Phase 1994 - 1996
(paragraphs 31 - 38)

The idea of the first phase
is to make all of us aware of
the importance of the Jubilee.

Christ is at the centre of these preparations.
Let us remember that the celebration of the Jubilee
is above all a celebration of him:

The Jubilee celebration should confirm
the Christians of today
*in their **faith** in God who has revealed himself in Christ, sustain*
*their **hope** which reaches out in expectation of eternal life,*
*and rekindle their **charity***
in active service to their brothers and sisters. (paragraph 31)

There will be a Committee in Rome for the Jubilee
and each local Church will have a Commission.

The Jubilee of the Year 2000 is meant to be
a great prayer of praise and thanksgiving,
especially for the gift
of the Incarnation of the Son of God
and of the Redemption which he accomplished. (paragraph 32)

3. The themes we are going to work

In the first place
we are going to meditate on the mystery
of the love of *God our Father,*
who gave us his Son.

In the second place
we are going to thank God
for the gift of the *Church* which unites us.

We are also going to thank him
for the testimony of the *holiness*
of so many of our brothers and sisters
who are living like saints.

In the third place
we are going to celebrate the gift of conversion:

The joy of every jubilee is above all
a joy based on forgiveness of sins,
the joy of conversion. (paragraph 32)

4. The importance of reconciliation

The theme of reconciliation
was dealt with by the bishops
in their Synod of 1984.

The Church everywhere has to undergo conversion,
the precondition for reconciliation with God.
We must admit with humility
those times when we have not only been selfish
but have caused scandal.

The Church should become more fully conscious
of the sinfulness of her children,
recalling all those times in history
when they departed from the spirit of Christ and his Gospel
and, instead of offering to the world the witness of
a life inspired by values of faith,
indulged in ways of thinking and acting
which were truly forms of counter-witness and scandal. (paragrap

The Dogmatic Constitution on the Church
Lumen Gentium
of the Second Vatican Council
said the same thing in *paragraph 8*:

The Church,
embracing sinners to her bosom,
is at the same time holy and always in need of being purified,
and incessantly pursues the path of penance and renewal.
(paragraph 33)

We cannot advance to the new millennium
without recognising our actual failings.

Acknowledging the weaknesses of the past
is an act of honesty and courage
which helps us to strengthen our faith,
which alerts us to face today's temptations
and challenges and prepares us to meet them. (paragraph 33)

Of what should the Church repent?
The Pope says there are many areas that require conversion.

5. The lack of unity among the churches

Among the sins which we should repent
are those which have been *detrimental to the unity
willed by God for his People. (paragraph 34)*
Tragically, the last thousand years
have been characterised by division and separation.

The truth is that people
on both sides were to blame.
Where the separation happened a long time ago
the temptation is to continue to aggravate the divisions
instead of healing them.

*In these last years of the millennium,
the Church should invoke the Holy Spirit
with ever greater insistence,
imploring the grace of Christian unity. (paragraph 34)*

It is certain that much has been done
in favour of Christian unity
and it is also one of the on-going tasks which we have to do.
But unity is, after all, the gift of the spirit.

Because of this, in these years leading up to the year 2000
we must examine our consciences
and look for opportunities for the
promotion of fitting ecumenical activities. (paragraph 34)

Although we may not reach unity

in the remaining years of this millennium,
nevertheless we must come as close as possible
to overcoming the divisions between Christians.
We can do this in part with dialogue and partnership
but above all through increased prayer.

6. The lack of tolerance and the use of violence

There is another failing
which we must recognise with humility:
In other eras in the history of the Church,
the Church has accepted intolerance and even violence,
supposedly in the service of truth.
But truth that is imposed by violence is not truth.

We must not judge those
who lived in the past
with the same criteria which we employ
today to condemn violence in our century.
Nevertheless, it is certain that hatreds of bygone times
have created a vicious circle which continues to affect us today.

The sons and daughters of the Church who have used violence
have sullied the face of the Church
so that it cannot reflect the true Christ.
At least from this sad reality
we can learn a lesson for the future.

The truth cannot impose itself
except by virtue of its own truth,
as it wins over the mind with both gentleness and power.
(paragraph 35)

You can read about this theme
in the Declaration on Religious Freedom *Dignitatis Humanae* of
  Second Vatican Council.

7. Religious indifference and injustice

It is not enough just to look at the faults of the past.
We must with great humility examine

our responsibility with regard to the evils of our own time.

To what extent are we responsible for the fact
that so many people have no or little interest in religion?
Many people in our century do not believe in God.
Some do not accept the dignity of the person
or fundamental values of respect for life and the family.
These ideas can also affect the members of the Church.
When we do not give a witness to our faith,
we do not reflect *the true face of God.*

Many are uncertain about morality,
about prayer and about their faith;
This is sometimes made worse by erroneous theology
and lack of obedience in the Church.

With respect to the Church of our time
how can we not lament the lack of discernment,
which at times became even acquiescence,
shown by many Christians
concerning the violation of fundamental human rights
by totalitarian regimes?
And should we not also regret,
among the shadows of our own day,
the responsibility shared by so many Christians
for grave forms of injustice and exclusion?
It must be asked how many Christians
really know and put into practice
the principles of the Church's social doctrine. (paragraph 36)

8. Have we assimilated the teachings of the Second Vatican Council into our lives?

Have we read and studied the Bible
as requested by the Constitution *Dei Verbum?*

Is the liturgy *"the origin and summit"* of our faith,
as the Constitution *Sacrosanctum Concilium* asks us?

Do we promote the different ministries and gifts

as the Constitution *Lumen Gentium* asks us?

Last year we celebrated the 30th anniversary
of *Gaudium et Spes.*
Have we kept open the dialogue
with men and women of goodwill so as
to work for justice and peace,
as proposed by *Gaudium et Spes*
which outlines the role of the Church in the Modern World?

9. Witness of life

When we study the history of the Church
we discover that the Church increased in size in the first centur
thanks to the courage of its members.
Many of them were martyrs:
that is, they gave their lives for the faith.

At the end of the second millennium,
the Church has once again
become a Church of martyrs. (paragraph 37)

In different parts of the world today
many Christians
- and not only Catholics -
have paid the supreme sacrifice for their faith.

As far as possible, their witness should not be lost to the Church
the local Churches should do everything possible
to ensure that the memory of those
who have suffered martyrdom should be safeguarded,
gathering the necessary documentation.
This gesture cannot fail to have an ecumenical character and
   expression.
Perhaps the most convincing form of ecumenism
is the ecumenism of the saints and of the martyrs. (paragraph 3

Not only by death do people give witness:
the best example of witness
that we can give is the practice of faith, hope and love.
Examples of these are given daily,
especially through those who are married.

10. The Synods (meetings) in each continent

It is now proposed to have Synods of bishops in every continent.

The bishops of **Africa** met in Rome in 1994.

The meeting of the bishops of **Latin America**
took place in Santo Domingo in 1992.
It is proposed to have a Synod for the Americas
on the themes
of evangelisation and justice
between the two parts of the continent, north and south.

There will also be a Synod for **Asia**
concerning the encounter
of Christianity with local cultures and religions,
particularly Buddhism and Hinduism.
At the time of the Great Jubilee
it would be good to reflect
on Christ as Mediator and Redeemer of the world.

A Synod for the countries of **Oceania**
could work on the encounter
of Christianity with the most ancient forms of religion.

QUESTIONS
to help us understand the text

In this part of the letter the Pope speaks to us about the preparation for the Jubilee, above all, about the current need to raise awareness.

Themes we must work on include reconciliation and conversion.

The Jubilees exist for the forgiveness of sins, and with humility we must admit our faults.

The Pope proposes various reflections:

In what way do we work for the unity of Christians?
Or have we given a bad example that scandalises others?
What can we do to work together with those who are not Catholics
to obtain justice and peace?

Can we think of examples where members of the Church have accepted intolerence and even violence supposedly in the service of the Church?
If the truth should commend itself because of its own merits and never because of violence, how should the Church witness to the truth?
Who suffers from violence that might need our help?

In our Christian communities have we studied the documents of the Second Vatican Council?
What have we done to implement the teachings of the Second Vatican Council?

Do we know cases of people who have given their lives for their faith - that is to say, are martyrs?
Tell their stories to your community.

What examples can we give of the practice of faith, hope and love in our everyday lives?

Can you give examples of how the family and marriage give witness to Christ?

B) SECOND PHASE *1997-1999*

(paragraphs 39-55)

The preparations now move on to the
Second Phase.
There will be special preparations
for each year: 1997, 1998 and 1999.
It will be a Trinitarian celebration. *(paragraph 39)*

1. The First Year - 1997
Dedicated to Jesus Christ

It will be centred in Christ,
The Word of God,
made man by the power of the Holy Spirit. (paragraph 40)

The general theme is:
Jesus Christ, the one Saviour of the world,
yesterday, today and forever. (paragraph 40)

The Incarnation of Jesus Christ
is what we will celebrate in the Jubilee.
We will underline especially what is said
in the gospel of St Luke (Lk 4:18-19):

"The Spirit of the Lord is upon me
for he has anointed me:
to bring the Good News to the poor,
to proclaim liberty to captives
and sight to the blind,
to let the oppressed go free,
to proclaim a year of favour of the Lord."

We have to return to celebrate
once again the way in which Jesus was born of the Virgin
    Mary in Bethlehem.

In order to recognise who Christ truly is,
Christians, especially in the course of this year,
should turn with renewed interest to the Bible,
and the liturgy. (paragraph 40)

In terms of the liturgy
we will give special emphasis
to the sacrament of baptism
because it is the foundation of the Christian life;
as St Paul says (Gal 3:27):

As many of you as were baptised into Christ
have put on Christ. (paragraph 41)

Baptism is also
that which unites us with other Christians who are not
    Catholics,
as we all share one baptism.

In this way the activities for 1997,
Christ,
the Word of God
and baptism, are motives to promote ecumenism.

In that way the principal object
of the Jubilee Year 2000 will be met:
the strengthening of faith
and of the witness of Christians. (paragraph 42)

This will be made clear in our own conversion
to the Lord and to our neighbour,
especially the most needy.

The first year therefore
will be the opportune moment
for a renewed appreciation of catechesis
in its original meaning as "the Apostles' teaching" (Acts 2:42)
about the person of Jesus Christ
and his mystery of salvation. (paragraph 42)

One practical proposal is that people be encouraged to study
the Catechism of the Catholic Church.

The mystery of Mary, Mother of Our Lord,
will also be celebrated during this preparation.

In the year 1997 dedicated to Jesus Christ
we will also study the Divine Motherhood:
in that the Word became flesh (Jn 1:14).
Mary is the model of living faith,
and when we meditate on her
we enter into the profound mystery of the Incarnation.

2. The Second Year - 1998
   ## Dedicated to the Holy Spirit

The mystery of the Incarnation of Jesus Christ
is realised through the work of the Holy Spirit,
and it is the Holy Spirit that sanctifies
the disciples of Christ.
If we want to celebrate the Jubilee Year 2000,
it will be by the power of that same Spirit.
Because it is the Spirit that makes real
the revelation of Christ to us.

The concrete objective of the year 1998 is therefore,
a renewed appreciation of the presence
and activity of the Spirit. (paragraph 45)
Amongst the sacraments
Confirmation best emphasises the role of the Spirit.
It is the Spirit who gives the gifts to each of us

43

and also obtains the unity of us all.

In our own day too,
the Spirit is the principal agent of the new evangelisation.
Hence it will be important to gain a renewed appreciation
of the Spirit as the One
who builds the Kingdom of God
within the course of history
and prepares its full manifestation in Jesus Christ,
stirring people's hearts and quickening in our world
the seeds of full salvation which will come at the end of
*   time. (paragraph 45)*

Because of this the virtue which characterises
the Kingdom of God is **hope**.

The basic attitude of hope, on the one hand
encourages the Christian
not to lose sight of the final goal
which gives meaning and value to life,
and on the other,
offers solid and profound reasons
for a daily commitment to transform reality
in order to make it
correspond to God's plan. (paragraph 46)
(Read Rom 8:22-24).

Christians are called to prepare
for the Great Jubilee of the beginning of the Third
*   Millennium*
by renewing their hope
in the definitive coming of the Kingdom of God,
preparing for it daily in their hearts,
in the Christian community to which they belong,
in their particular social context,
and in world history itself. (paragraph 46)

When we look at the end of this century,
although we see many things that are going badly,
there also exist signs of hope.
For example, medical progress in the service of human life,

a greater awareness of our responsibility for the environment
and efforts to obtain peace, justice, reconciliation
and solidarity between the countries of North and South.

We also see signs of hope in the Church:
for example, the importance which is given now
to create and develop a lay Church,
to work for unity amongst Christians,
and inter-religious dialogue and dialogue with cultures.

In effect, the special task for 1998
must be to be aware of and alert
to the *value of unity within the Church. (paragraph 47)*
The Dogmatic Constitution on the Church,
Lumen Gentium of the Second Vatican Council
said that *the unity of the Body of Christ
is founded on the activity of the Spirit. (paragraph 47)*

We know we are going to celebrate Mary
during these three years of preparation.
In this year 1998, dedicated to the Holy Spirit,
we remember how Jesus was conceived
by the work and grace of the Spirit.
We can see Mary therefore
as a woman who was responsive to the Spirit,
who gave full expression to the longing of the poor of
    Yahweh, a woman of hope.

3. *The Third Year - 1999*
Dedicated to God the Father

Jesus Christ had a vision of his Father
as the One who wants to give us the gift of eternal life.
The goal of this year and of always
is that we Christians gain that same vision.

The Gospel according to John (17:3)
tells us all about this vision:

*This is eternal life, that they know you the only true God,
and Jesus Christ whom you have sent. (paragraph 49)*

45

We as Christians and all humanity
are on this way towards the house of God.

The Jubilee, centred on Christ,
is like a prayer of praise to the Father.

If we are on a journey to the Father
then we have to go through a conversion -
a change of heart,
a change away from sin,
a change towards good, which the gospel teaches.

Because of that,
the sacrament which we are going to celebrate in 1999
is that of Reconciliation, also known as Penance.
Without reconciliation
it is not possible for human love to exist.

Just as we celebrate faith in 1997
and hope in 1998,
in 1999 we are going to celebrate the virtue of charity,
for God is love.
Love summarises all of Christian law.
(Read the First Letter of St John 4:8,16.)

4. The preferential option for the poor

The Gospel of St Matthew (11:5)
says to us that Jesus came
to *preach the good news to the poor.*
From this point of view,
*how can we fail to lay greater emphasis
on the Church's preferential option for the poor and the
    outcast?*

*Indeed, it has to be said
that a commitment to justice and peace
in a world like ours,
marked by so many conflicts and intolerable social and
    economic inequalities,
is a necessary condition for*

the preparation and celebration of the Jubilee.
(paragraph 51)

5. The cancellation of debts and the external debt

The Book of Leviticus (25:8-28)
describes in detail how the Jubilee should be celebrated.
We must enter into that same spirit and be a voice for the
poor.

John Paul II has a specific proposal:
Christians will have to raise their voice
on behalf of all the poor of the world,
proposing the Jubilee as an appropriate time
to give thought, among other things,
to reducing substantially, if not cancelling outright,
the international debt
which seriously threatens the future of many nations.
(paragraph 51)

6. Other themes to reflect on

Other themes which we must also reflect on are:
the difficulties of dialogue between different cultures
and the problems connected with respect for women's rights
and the promotion of the family and marriage.
(paragraph 51)

Christ is the revelation of the Father
and he also reveals to us who we are and what is our
vocation.
Because of this, two other commitments are important:
meeting the challenge of secularism
and dialogue with the great religions. (paragraph 52)

What does "secularism" mean?
It is when the world advances from the standpoint of
technology
but people forget about God;
it is when people believe they are self-sufficient
and think that they no longer need religion.

This crisis of civilisation must be countered
by the civilisation of love,
founded on the universal values
of peace, solidarity, justice and liberty,
which find their full attainment in Christ. (paragraph 52)

The other theme is inter-religious dialogue
as set out in the Second Vatican Council's Declaration
on relations with non-Christian religions *(Nostra Aetate)*.
Two religious groups in particular
with whom we must dialogue
are the Jews and the Muslims.
God grant that as a confirmation of these intentions
it may also be possible to hold joint meetings
in places of significance for the great monotheistic religions.
(paragraph 53)

In this year we must also remember Mary
who is the perfect model of love towards both God and
neighbour. (paragraph 54)

Read the prayer of praise of Mary that is called the
   Magnificat.
It is in the Gospel of Luke (1:46-55).
There we read how the Lord has done great things to her.
The Father chose her
for a unique mission in the history of salvation:
that of being the Mother of the long-awaited Saviour.
(paragraph 54)
Her presence will be felt during this year
as a loving invitation to all God's children
to return to the house of the Father.

QUESTIONS
to help us understand the text

In this section of the letter about the Jubilee
the Pope talks to us about the immediate preparations
   for the year 2000.
It is going to be a trinitarian celebration:

The year **1997** is centred on **Jesus Christ**:
we will celebrate the sacrament of **baptism**.
The virtue to take into account will be **faith**,
and activities concerned with **renewed interest in the
   Bible**, **ecumenism** and **catechetics**.

The year **1998** will be centred on the **Holy Spirit**:
We will celebrate the sacrament of **confirmation**.
The virtue to take into account will be **hope**
and the special activities will be
to look for signs of hope
that show the presence of the **Kingdom of God**
and work that shows the **unity of the Church**.

The year **1999** will be centred on God the **Father**:
where we will celebrate the sacrament of **reconciliation**.
The virtue to look for will be **charity**
and activites will be based mostly around
the **preferential option for the poor**
and the **commitment to justice and peace**.

Look through the ideas mentioned in the text.
Which of them would you like to see taken forward?

What specific ideas could be developed for years 1997,
   1998 and 1999?

Can you identify signs of hope locally, at diocesan level
   and nationally that strengthen belief in the coming of
   God's Kingdom?

QUESTIONS
to help us understand the text

What do you understand by the term, "preferential option for the poor"?

How can you work for the preferential option for the poor and a commitment to justice and peace?

One of the great problems which justice is facing is the question of international debt. In what ways can work be done towards relieving it?

c) Approaching the Celebration

(paragraph 55)

In summarised form,
these three years of preparation
look at one mystery
that is, the Holy Trinity,
from Christ and through Christ,
in the Holy Spirit, to the Father. (paragraph 55)

We are going to celebrate the year 2000
simultaneously
in the Holy Land, in Rome
and in each local Church.

To be able to celebrate
that Christ is the unique way to the Father,
in the year 2000 in Rome there will be
an International Eucharistic Conference.

As he did the first time in Bethlehem
the Saviour who *took flesh in Mary's womb twenty centuries
    ago,*
*continues to offer himself to humanity as a source of divine
    life,*
through the sacrament of the Eucharist. (paragraph 55)

Equally, to celebrate the ecumenical spirit of the Great
    Jubilee,
in the year 2000 there will also be a meeting of all
    Christians,

that is to say a gathering
in cooperation with Christians of other denominations and
    traditions,
as well as of grateful openness to those religions whose
    representatives
might wish to acknowledge
the joy shared by all the disciples of Christ. (paragraph 55)

The important thing is not to fail
to take advantage of this great goal which is the Jubilee.
This task is not just for the few but is in the hands of all of
    us.

QUESTIONS
to help us understand the text

There are many ways to prepare ourselves
and the Pope says that we must open ourselves
to the grace of the Spirit
so that each Christian community
can take on the work of the Great Jubilee.

There could be many possible activities.
In the end choices will have to be made locally
and the challenge will then be to put them into practice.
Keep alert to relevant initiatives going on already.

What suggestions could be fed into diocesan and
    national level planning?

What ecumenical possibilities are there locally, at
    diocesan level and nationally?

'JESUS CHRIST IS THE SAME ... FOREVER"
LETTER TO THE HEBREWS 13:8)

)aragraphs 56-59)

1. The Jubilee is like a parable

Do you remember the parable of the mustard seed?
Read it in the Gospel of St Matthew (13:31-32).
In the last 2000 years
the Church has grown just like the small mustard seed
and become a great tree.
The tree now covers all of humanity,
although not all are members of the Church.

Another parable in the Gospel of St Matthew
is that of the leaven (13:33).
Christ, like a divine leaven,
always and ever more fully penetrates the life of humanity,
spreading the work of salvation
accomplished in the Paschal Mystery. (paragraph 56)

As the text from the Letter to the Hebrews says (Heb 13:8):
"Jesus Christ is the same yesterday and today and forever."
Jesus is present in our past and in our future.

53

2. The evangelisation of all the world

The mission of the Church
has been continuous from the time of Christ until today.
In the first millennium evangelisation happened in Europe
    and made its way to Asia.
The evangelisation of the American continent began some
    500 years ago.
Although there had been missionaries in Africa from the
    beginning,
the missionary activity in that continent grew tremendously
    in the last 100 years.
With the fall of the great anti-Christian systems in Europe
there is need here too
of the liberating message of the Gospel once more.

In the Second Vatican Council
the bishops wrote a special document
called *Ad Gentes*
(which means "The Mission to the Peoples").

Recent popes have also spoken on this theme:
Paul VI wrote *Evangelii Nuntiandi* in 1975,
(which means "The Evangelisation of the Peoples").

John Paul II wrote *Redemptoris Missio* in 1990
(which means "The Mission of the Redeemer").

John Paul II says today
we have to take the word of Christ
to the cultures of our world
and into politics and into economics as well.

3. Young people as agents of evangelisation

Who are going to be the agents of evangelisation?
The young people who are born in this century
will be the evangelisers after the year 2000.
Remember the conversation of Christ
with the young person
in the Gospel of St Matthew (19:16):

Christ expects great things from young people,
as he did from the young man who asked him:
"What good deed must I do, to have eternal life?"
(paragraph 58)

Christ invites all young people today
to join in the mission of evangelisation
for today, for tomorrow and until the end of the world.

The Pope ends his letter about the Jubilee
by recalling once more
the Pastoral Constitution on the Church in the Modern
   World
of the Second Vatican Council, *Gaudium et Spes*:

Christ continues to give us the strength of his Spirit
to carry on and complete our historical vocation
of being each day more human:
because in the most benign Lord and Master can be found
the key,
the focal point,
and the goal of all human history. (paragraph 59)

So from Christ the Church is able to collaborate
in the *finding of solutions*
to the outstanding problems of our times. *(paragraph 59)*

The Pope calls Christian communities
to open themselves to the Spirit,
to discern how to celebrate the Jubilee
and he gives us this great work
and asks Mary, the Mother of our Redeemer,
to intercede for us.

QUESTIONS
to help us understand the text

In what ways can we take the word of Christ into the cultures of our world and into politics and into economics as well?

How can young people join in the mission of evangelisation into the first century of the new millennium?